COLLINS GEM

C36 **Classic** £1·00

FILMS

Simon Rose

D1395586

HarperCollins*Publishers*

Critic Simon Rose reviews movies for *Sunday Business* and *Sky News*. He is the author of the *Essential Film Guide* and the *Classic Film Guide*. This selection is taken from the *Classic Film Guide*.

All pictures supplied courtesy of The Kobal Collection. Credits listed on p 192.

The author and publishers have made every reasonable effort to contact all copyright holders. Any errors that may have occurred are inadvertent and anyone who for any reason has not been contacted is invited to write to the publishers so that a full acknowledgement may be made in subsequent editions of this work.

HarperCollins Publishers
PO Box, Glasgow G4 0NB

First published 1999

Reprint 10 9 8 7 6 5 4 3 2 1 0

© Simon Rose 1999

ISBN 0 00 472329-5

Printed in Italy by Amadeus S.p.A.

Contents

Introduction

Selecting just under a hundred films to represent the best of cinema through the years is a horrendous task. Few people are likely to agree with every choice. But while you may have at least half-a-dozen candidates for movies you are convinced should have been in this book, can you really find fault with any that are included?

These films were chosen, not to please film buffs, but rather the average movie fan. Too many so-called 'classic' films look antiquated to contemporary viewers, with clunky dialogue, hammy acting and leaden direction. Not so these movies. They are chosen because they appear as fresh today as when they were made. Whether old or more recent, these celluloid marvels still have the power to move, enlighten, and above all, to entertain – whether it be the sheer entertainment value of films like *The Adventures of Robin Hood* and *Goldfinger*, the power of epics like *Schindler's List* and *The Godfather* or the antics and hilarity of films like *A Hard Day's Night* and *A Night at the Opera*.

Anyone wanting to start a collection of classic movies could do no better than to begin with those in this book.

The Adventures of Robin Hood

(1938)

Only The Rainbow Can Duplicate its Brilliance

Director: Michael Curtiz & William Keighley

Length: 102 min   **Rating:** U

Source: The novel Ivanhoe by Sir Walter Scott &
opera Robin Hood by R De Koven & Harry B. Smith

Sir Robin of Locksley	Errol Flynn
Maid Marian	Olivia De Havilland
Sir Guy of Gisbourne	Basil Rathbone
Prince John	Claude Rains
Will Scarlett	Patric Knowles
Friar Tuck	Eugene Pallette
Little John	Alan Hale
High Sheriff of Nottingham	Melville Cooper
King Richard	Ian Hunter

Accept no substitutes. This is the greatest
swashbuckling adventure of them all, with Flynn the
dashing Robin and his merry band of character actors
taking on the dastardly Rathbone and wooing the lovely
De Havilland. Exciting, funny, romantic, beautifully
cast and filmed, the whole delicious mix is topped off
with rousing music from the great Korngold. This one
should be in every video collection.

- At the time the film cost $1.9 million, making it Warners' most expensive film.

- When Will Scarlett goes to help Much, the miller's son, a car is visible in the background as he gets off his horse.

- Flynn did many of his own stunts, including duelling with Rathbone, who was probably the best swordsman in Hollywood. In one scene, Rathbone was injured by a spear and needed eight stitches in his foot.

'You speak treason' – 'Fluently'

Question: *Where was Sherwood Forest filmed?*

The African Queen

(1951)

Director: John Huston

Screenplay: James Agee

Length: 103 min   **Rating:** U

Source: Novel by C.S. Forester

Charlie Allnut ....Humphrey Bogart
Rose Sayer ....Katharine Hepburn
Rev. Samuel Sayer ....Robert Morley
German captain ....Peter Bull
German 1st officer ....Theodore Bikel
German 2nd officer ....Walter Gotell

During World War I, a starchy missionary and a hard-drinking trader are forced to live together on the same boat, enduring a perilous journey down river. One of the great adventure stories of all time, with both leads divine as the couple whose mutual hate turns first into respect and then love. A mite self-indulgent in places perhaps, it's still extremely witty and involving, the action sequences are suitably thrilling and the photography makes the hardships of filming in Africa look well worthwhile. Unfortunately, the stuff filmed on set in London jars because it looks so glaringly obvious.

- Bogart won his only Oscar for the film.

- Most of the company came down with dysentery. After lambasting Bogart and Huston for their heavy drinking and showing them up by drinking water with her meals, Hepburn realized that it was their abhorrence of water that kept them free of the disease that made her feel she was going to die.

- The novel *White Hunter, Black Heart*, made into a movie by Clint Eastwood, was based on those who made *The African Queen*.

'By the authority vested in me by Kaiser Wilhelm II, I pronounce you man and wife. Proceed with the execution.'

Question: *Which two earlier American films were made on location in Africa?*

All About Eve

(1950)

Director: Joseph L. Mankiewicz

Length: 138 min   **Rating:** U

Source: Story, *The Wisdom of Eve* by Mary Orr

Margo Channing	Bette Davis
Eve Harrington	Anne Baxter
Addison DeWitt	George Sanders
Karen Richards	Celeste Holm
Bill Simpson	Gary Merrill
Lloyd Richards	Hugh Marlowe
Birdie	Thelma Ritter
Miss Casswell	Marilyn Monroe
Max Fabian	Gregory Ratoff

In an untypical moment of weakness a temperamental star befriends a star-struck fan, only to find that she is really a ruthless monster. One of the bitchiest, most caustically witty films ever to hit the screen, brought vividly to life by a cast acting their little cotton socks off. A source of endless joy, with a fascinating early appearance by Monroe as an aspiring actress.

- The film's 14 Oscar nominations have never been bettered, though it won only six of them.

- Although author Orr claims the original story was based on actress Elisabeth Bergner, others are convinced that Davis based her character on her rival Tallulah Bankhead.

- Davis and Merrill, who had never met before filming began, fell in love during the production and married a month and half after filming finished. They divorced 10 years later.

> 'Bill's 32. He looks 32. He looked it 5 years ago. He'll look it 20 years from now. I hate men.'

Question: *Who was originally meant to play the part of Margo Channing?*

All Quiet on the Western Front

(1930)

Director: Lewis Milestone

Length: 140 min   **Rating:** PG

Source: Novel by Erich Maria Remarque

Paul Baumer	Lew Ayres
Katczinsky	Louis Wolheim
Himmelstoss	John Wray
Gerard Duval	Raymond Griffith
Tjaden	Slim Summerville
Muller	Russell Gleason
Kemmerick	Ben Alexander
Mrs. Baumer	Beryl Mercer

One of the greatest cinematic arguments against war still has enormous power to move today, even if some of the methods used to relate the story appear somewhat archaic now. Told from the German point of view, it follows a group of keen recruits overtaken by the nightmare that was World War I. It's a depressing film, but most definitely a worthwhile experience.

- Future director Fred Zinnemann, who was to make movies like *High Noon* and *The Day of the Jackal*, appears here as an extra.

- There was pressure from the producers for a happy ending. Fed up of arguing, Milestone once told them: 'I've got your happy ending. We'll let the Germans win the war.'

- The film was denounced by Goebbels as anti-German, but the Poles banned it for being pro-German. In France it was prohibited until 1962.

> 'We live in the trenches out there. We fight. We try not to be killed. But sometimes we are. That's all.'

Question: *How were the realistic war scenes set?*

American Graffiti

(1973)

'Where Were You In '62?'

Director: George Lucas

Length: 110 min   **Rating:** PG

Source: Autobiographical

Curt Henderson	Richard Dreyfuss
Steve Bolander	Ron Howard
John Milner	Paul LeMat
Terry Fields	Charles Martin Smith
Laurie	Cindy Williams
Debbie	Candy Clark
Falfa	Harrison Ford
Carol	Mackenzie Phillips
Himself	Wolfman Jack
Joe	Bo Hopkins
Peg	Kathleen Quinlan
Blonde in T-Bird	Suzanne Somers

A group of teenagers cruise around their small town in the early 60s. This influential coming-of-age movie, backed by fabulous music, is witty, entertaining and great, great fun. Based on Lucas' own experiences growing up in Modesto, California, we end up being terribly envious that we weren't there at the same time as him.

- Universal's executives were unimpressed by the idea of the project and after the premiere threatened not to release it, even though the response from the audience was superb.

- The movie, filmed over just 29 days, cost only $750,000 and went on to make over $100m. Its success meant Lucas could make *Star Wars*.

- The cinema is showing *Dementia 13*, the first movie co-producer Francis Ford Coppola made.

- The soundtrack of nostalgic pop hits blazed a trail. The rights for the songs used cost 10% of the entire budget.

Question: *What is the significance of the number plate on the car?*

Annie Hall

(1977)

Director: Woody Allen

Length: 93 min   **Rating:** 15

Alvy Singer	Woody Allen
Annie Hall	Diane Keaton
Rob	Tony Roberts
Allison	Carol Kane
Tony Lacey	Paul Simon
Pam	Shelley Duvall
Mom Hall	Colleen Dewhurst
Duane Hall	Christopher Walken
Robin	Janet Margolin
TV show actress	Beverly D'Angelo

The story of a troubled relationship between a neurotic New York Jewish gag-writer and a flibbertigibbet wannabe singer, with the worst taste in clothes since Abraham Lincoln. Insightful into the problems of dating and living together, it is also extremely funny for much of its length. There are also some more languid stretches, though, and you can't help feeling on occasion that knocking their heads together would achieve rather more than all that jawing.

- Allen seems almost proud of the fact that no other Oscar-winning film has made so little at the box office, taking $36m at the box office worldwide.

- The film is pretty clearly based on Allen's former relationship with Diane Keaton. Hall was her real surname. Allan, however, denies this.

- Keep awake and you might spot Jeff Goldblum at the party in LA and Sigourney Weaver in her film debut as Allen's date in the cinema queue at the end.

> 'I was thrown out of NYU my freshman year for cheating on my metaphysics final. I looked into the soul of the boy sitting next to me.'

Question: *What was Woody Allen doing the night his movie won 4 Oscars?*

The Apartment
(1960)

Director: Billy Wilder

Length: 125 min   **Rating:** PG

C.C. 'Bud' Baxter .Jack Lemmon

Fran Kubelik .Shirley MacLaine

J.D. Sheldrake . . . . .Fred MacMurray

Joe Dobisch . . . . .Ray Walston

Al Kirkeby . . . . .David Lewis

Dr Dreyfuss . . . . .Jack Kruschen

Sylvia . . . . .Joan Shawlee

Miss Olsen . . . . .Edie Adams

Lemmon is a slightly pathetic insurance guy climbing the ladder less through his efforts at work than through his willingness to let his apartment be used by his seniors for conducting office affairs. When lift-girl MacLaine is dumped by one of them, Lemmon has to decide whether he's a man or a mouse. This delicious bitter-sweet comedy is a must.

• Wilder had promised Lemmon a honey of a part in return for dressing up in drag in *Some Like It Hot*. This was it.

• *The Apartment* won 3 Oscars.

• Paul Douglas was originally going to play Fred MacMurray's role, but he fell ill and died just two

weeks before the production got under way.

- No-one knew the ending in advance, including the writers. The actors got the pages for the final scene less than half an hour before they were due to film it. They did it in one take.

- The film was turned into a Broadway musical, *Promises, Promises*, in 1968.

> 'When you're in love with a married man, you shouldn't wear mascara.'

Question: *Shirley MacLaine has a habit that drove Billy Wilder crazy. What was it?*

Apocalypse Now

(1979)

Director: Francis Ford Coppola

Length: 153 min   **Rating:** 18

Source: inspired by Joseph Conrad's novel *Heart of Darkness*

Col. Kurtz	Marlon Brando
Lt. Col. Kilgore	Robert Duvall
Capt. Willard	Martin Sheen
Chef	Frederic Forrest
Chief	Albert Hall
Lance	Sam Bottoms
Clean	Laurence Fishburne
Photojournalist	Dennis Hopper
Colonel	Harrison Ford
General	G.D. Spradlin
Colby (civilian)	Scott Glenn

During the Vietnam War, a captain is sent up river into Cambodia to kill a colonel who has gone native. This extraordinary and unforgettable movie, bizarre and quirky in the extreme, is filled with memorable scenes. However, it isn't a coherent whole and becomes incredibly confusing towards the close. Inspired by Joseph Conrad's novel *Heart of Darkness*, try to catch the documentary made by Coppola's wife Eleanor,

Hearts of Darkness, which shows the fascinating background to the making of the film.

- Filming in the Philippines did not go smoothly. Hurricane Olga wrecked the sets completely, the 24 helicopters lent by Ferdinand Marcos' government kept being commandeered to have a go at rebels and Sheen had a heart attack.

- Duvall's helicopter attack on the village actually blew up the production's prop and paint shop.

- The killing of the ox was part of a local native ceremony that Coppola filmed and popped into the movie.

Question: *What was this film's nickname?*

Arsenic and Old Lace
(1944)

Director: Frank Capra

Length: 118 min   **Rating:** PG

Source: Play by Joseph Kesselring

Mortimer Brewster	....................Cary Grant
Elaine Harper	........................Priscilla Lane
Jonathan Brewster	.............Raymond Massey
Dr Einstein	...........................Peter Lorre
Abby Brewster	....................Josephine Hull
Martha Brewster	.......................Jean Adair
Officer O'Hara	........................Jack Carson
Mr. Witherspoon	..........Edward Everett Horton
Lt. Rooney	........................James Gleason
'Teddy' Brewster	.................John Alexander

Two old ladies take pity on men suffering from loneliness – by poisoning them! Nephew Cary Grant finds out what's going on and nearly breaks his neck doing rapid double-takes. Then the even more psychopathic Massey turns up. Although barely changed from the stage version, this is a delicious farcical black comedy which fairly hums along.

• Capra was about to go into the Signal Corps and wanted a quick movie to keep his family while he was away. He got a leave of absence so that he could finish filming.

- Preview audiences were disgusted that Edward Everett Horton also succumbed to the ladies. It was rapidly changed.

- The censors wouldn't wear the last line of the play, which had the delighted Grant saying: 'Do you understand? I'm a bastard!' 'I'm the son of a sea cook' isn't quite the same.

- When Grant is sitting on a tombstone, one of the headstones says 'Archie Leach', his real name.

> 'One of our gentlemen found time to say 'How delicious!' before he died...'

Question: *What year was this film actually made?*

Ben Hur

(1959)

Director: William Wyler

Length: 212 min   **Rating:** PG

Source: Novel by Lew Wallace

Judah Ben Hur	Charlton Heston
Quintus Arrius	Jack Hawkins
Messala	Stephen Boyd
Esther	Haya Harareet
Sheik Ilderim	Hugh Griffith
Miriam	Martha Scott
Simonides	Sam Jaffe
Tirzah	Cathy O'Donnell
Balthasar	Finlay Currie
Pilate	Frank Thring
Emperor Tiberius	George Relph

This epic tale is once seen, never forgotten, thanks to the grandiosely-staged galley fight and the chariot races. In an age that pays some actors more than this movie cost, we can but marvel at the days when it was still possible to put such incredible spectacles on celluloid. The original 1925 silent version is also pretty exciting in places.

- At the time, the most expensive film ever made, with a cost of almost $15m. The movie nearly sent MGM into

bankruptcy, but the film was phenomenally successful, grossing $40 million. Its clutch of 11 Oscars was a record.

- Stuntman Yakima Canutt, organised the chariot race. Heston and Boyd did many of their own stunts and, while Heston was already an experienced handler of horses, Boyd had a far harder time of it, with bloody, blistered hands and severe bruising from the scene where he's dragged underneath his chariot.

- All the Romans are played by Brits while the Jews are all American.

> 'Your God, in His eagerness to save you, has also saved the Roman fleet.'

Question: *Why did Stephen Boyd have to wear dark contact lenses for the role of Messala?*

The Best Years of Our Lives
(1946)

Director: William Wyler

Length: 172 min   **Rating:** U

Source: Article in *Time* magazine & *Glory For Me* by MacKinlay Kantor

Milly Stephenson	Myrna Loy
Al Stephenson	Fredric March
Fred Derry	Dana Andrews
Peggy Stephenson	Teresa Wright
Marie Derry	Virginia Mayo
Wilma Cameron	Cathy O'Donnell
Butch Engle	Hoagy Carmichael
Homer Parrish	Harold Russell
Hortense Derry	Gladys George

Three veterans of World War II return to their homes and try to readjust to civilian life and the casual attitude so many Americans had to the sacrifices servicemen made on their behalf. This beautifully made film still manages to make us extremely angry, as it was meant to do. The outstanding cast manipulate our emotions expertly, wringing our withers one moment and making us gloriously happy the next. Cinematic story-telling at its very best.

- MacKinlay Kantor was asked to write a short treatment. He came back after three months with a 268-page work, *Glory for Me*, written in free verse. Even when he was given more money to turn it into a screenplay, what was handed in was virtually unusable.

- To get Russell – a Canadian war veteran – worked up for his tussle with Ray Teal, Wyler told him that Teal was a closet Fascist and watched the sparks fly.

- Wyler made the actors use their own clothes throughout, wanting a lack of glamour.

'I don't care if it doesn't make a nickel. I just want every man, woman and child in America to see it.' [Producer Sam Goldwyn]

Question: *What is unusual about Russell's Oscars?*

The Big Sleep

(1946)

Director: Howard Hawks

Length: 114 min   **Rating:** PG

Source: Novel by Raymond Chandler

Philip Marlowe	Humphrey Bogart
Vivian Rutledge	Lauren Bacall
Eddie Mars	John Ridgeley
Carmen Sternwood	Martha Vickers
Joe Brody	Louis Jean Heydt
Jones	Elisha Cook Jr.
Bernie Ohis	Regis Toomey
Proprietess	Dorothy Malone
Gen. Sternwood	Charles Waldron
Norris	Charles D. Brown

One of the greatest of all detective movies, with Bogart's Philip Marlowe coping with smutty photos, murder and blackmail. True, it's sometimes hard to work out exactly what's going on. But there are enormous pleasures to be had from this richly-textured film noir, such as Bogie's seen-it-all gumshoe, the sparks flying between him and Bacall and the wry, witty and often surprisingly sexy dialogue. A classic that well deserves the accolade.

- Bogart and Bacall had been married for almost a year when *The Big Sleep* came out, although Hawks had tried to persuade his protegé Bacall that the relationship could damage her movie career.

- Hawks claimed later that 'I never figured out what was going on, but I though that the basic thing had great scenes in it and it was good entertainment. After that got by, I said, "I'm never going to worry about being logical again".'

> 'I don't mind if you don't like my manners. I don't like them myself. They're pretty bad. I grieve over them on long winter evenings.'

Question: *What mystery did Hawks want Raymond Chandler to solve?*

Blade Runner
(1982)

Director: Ridley Scott

Length: 116 min   **Rating:** 15

Source: Short story, *Do Androids Dream of Electric Sheep?* by Philip K. Dick

Deckard	Harrison Ford
Batty	Rutger Hauer
Rachel	Sean Young
Gaff	Edward James Olmos
Bryant	M. Emmet Walsh
Pris	Daryl Hannah
Leon	Brion James
Zhora	Joanna Cassidy

Ridley Scott's exciting, stylish futuristic thriller is regarded as one of the best and most influential sci-fi pics ever. The original release had an explanatory voiceover and implausible happy ending imposed on it. A director's cut was released in 1992. Both are brilliant. Ford's job is to 'retire' rogue androids but his dedication to the job wavers when he gets a close look at Sean Young. Disturbingly, the once amazingly futuristic look of the film looks considerably less fantastical over a decade later, as reality moves closer to Scott's bleak vision of city life to come.

- When Zhora goes through the glass, it's clearly not her doing the stunt, besides which she's wearing something more solid than the bikini she put on just before.

- Ford's part was at one time a possibility for Dustin Hoffman, while Philip K. Dick, author of the original short story, was keen on Victoria Principal playing Sean Young's part!

- When the film went over budget, the happy ending (in the original version) used an outtake from the opening of *The Shining* as its backdrop.

'More human than human, is our motto.'

Question: *How many replicants escaped?*

Bonnie and Clyde

(1967)

They're Young...They're In Love...And They Kill People!

Director: Arthur Penn

Length: 111 min   **Rating:** 18

Source: Screenplay by David Newman & Robert Benton

Clyde Barrow . . . . .Warren Beatty
Bonnie Parker . . . . .Faye Dunaway
C.W. Moss . . . . .Michael J. Pollard
Buck Barrow .Gene Hackman
Blanche Barrow . . . . .Estelle Parsons
Eugene Grizzard . . . . .Gene Wilder
Capt. Frank Hamer . . . . .Denver Pyle
Ivan Moss . . . . .Dub Taylor

In the midst of the Depression, a pair of outlaws part a series of banks from their cash, caring little who gets in the way of their guns. There's a startling array of cinematic techniques on display here, as the photogenic pair are transformed into modern day Robin Hoods. Although some of the flashiness now irritates and marks it firmly as a product of the 60s, this innovative thriller is still one of the all-time great gangster movies.

- This was the first movie to make use of slow-motion violence.

- Hugely influenced by French New Wave filmmaking styles, Jean-Luc Godard and François Truffaut turned down the chance to direct, although they both made creative suggestions. It was Truffaut mentioning the project to Beatty that got him interested in the first place.

- Although they were no longer in business, the filmmakers used three of the actual banks in Texas that had been robbed by Bonnie and Clyde.

> 'We rob banks.'

Question: *Why was Warner's sued over this movie?*

Breakfast at Tiffany's
(1961)

Director: Blake Edwards

Length: 115 min   **Rating:** PG

Source: Novella by Truman Capote

Holly Golightly	Audrey Hepburn
Paul Varjak	George Peppard
2E	Patricia Neal
Doc Golightly	Buddy Ebsen
O.J. Berman	Martin Balsam
Mr. Yunioshi	Mickey Rooney
Tiffany's clerk	John McGiver
Sally Tomato	Alan Reed

Capote's novella of the enigmatic Holly Golightly, living off a succession of $50 bills given to her for the powder room by her gentleman friends, is here turned into gloriously sentimental moonshine. Hepburn has the same mesmerising effect on audiences as her character does in the movie, while the dialogue is top notch. The only drawback is the excruciatingly awful appearance of slant-eyed Rooney as her irascible Japanese neighbour. The stereotype is bad enough. The slapstick is worse.

- Hepburn is bare-legged when she crawls through Peppard's bedroom window. When she's sitting on his bed, she's got black stockings on.

'She's a phony, all right, but a real phony.'

Question: *What title did the studio want to give this movie?*

Brief Encounter

(1945)

Director: David Lean

Length: 86 min   **Rating:** PG

Source: Play, *Still Life* by Noël Coward

Laura Johnson	Celia Johnson
Alec Harvey	Trevor Howard
Albert Godby	Stanley Holloway
Myrtle Bagot	Joyce Carey
Fred Jesson	Cyril Raymond
Stephen Lynn	Valentine Dyall
Dolly Messiter	Everley Gregg
Boatman	Jack May
Organist	Irene Handl

This most exquisite of all British love stories goes against all the rules of popular cinema, featuring a far from exciting middle-aged, middle-class, couple – a housewife and a doctor – meeting by chance in a depressing railway station and falling head over heels for each other. But both are married and so it becomes clear that stiff upper lips will be called for. Unbearably poignant, yet not without humour, this is one of those rare films that can be watched again and again.

- The film was not a box office success at the time, despite winning the top prize at the Cannes Film Festival. After one preview produced hysterical laughter, Lean wanted to set the negative on fire and forget the whole project.

- The music is Rachmaninoff's Second Piano Concerto.

- Throughout his career Howard insisted on a clause in his contract allowing him to stay away from work while cricket test matches were being played.

> 'I believe we would be so different if we lived in a warm climate. We wouldn't be so shy and withdrawn and difficult.'

Question: *Where was this movie filmed?*

Cabaret

(1972)

A Divinely Decadent Experience

Director: Bob Fosse

Length: 124 min   **Rating:** 15

Source: Play by Joe Masteroff, play, *I Am a Camera* by John Van Druten & writings of Christopher Isherwood

Sally Bowles	Liza Minnelli
Brian Roberts	Michael York
Master of Ceremonies	Joel Grey
Maximillian von Heune	Helmut Griem
Fritz Wendel	Fritz Wepper
Natalia Landauer	Marisa Berenson

An Englishman in Berlin in the early 30s gets involved with an American, who's a singer in a trashy nightclub, and a German aristocrat. The rise of Nazism, and all it involved, is beautifully counterpointed with the songs performed at the Kit Kat Klub. Minnelli, in her greatest screen role, is really far too good to be the untalented Sally Bowles but we aren't complaining. Grey is also outstanding as the distinctly discomforting club MC.

- Bob Fosse, Joel Grey and Liza Minnelli won three of the film's eight Oscars.

- Minnelli's wardrobe came from German charity shops that she plundered to find sufficiently tacky clothes.

- The Nazi song 'Tomorrow Belongs to Me' was cut from the film when it was shown in Germany, perhaps sensible in the light of the anti-Semitism that Minnelli and other members of the cast and crew encountered there.

> 'Leave your troubles outside. Life is disappointing? In here, life is beautiful.'

Question: *Minnelli modelled her hair style on which 1928 film character?*

Casablanca

(1942)

As Big And Timely A Picture As Ever You've Seen! You Can Tell By The Cast It's Important! Gripping! Big!

Director: Michael Curtiz

Length: 102 min   **Rating:** U

Source: Play, *Everybody Comes to Rick's* by Murray Burnett & Joan Alison.

Rick Blaine	Humphrey Bogart
Ilsa Lund	Ingrid Bergman
Victor Laszlo	Paul Henreid
Capt. Louis Renault	Claude Rains
Maj. Heinrich Strasser	Conrad Veidt
Senor Ferrari	Sydney Greenstreet
Ugarte	Peter Lorre
Carl, headwaiter	S.Z. 'Cuddles' Sakall
Yvonne	Madeleine LeBeau
Sam	Dooley Wilson

Casablanca has got everything – melodrama, thrills, romance, comedy, politics – blended together into a perfect mixture. A tale of a resistance leader, a bar owner and the woman they both love thrown together in wartime North Africa, it is one of those rare films that gets better with every viewing. In large part this is due not only to the leads, but to a splendid supporting cast.

- Although taller than her when they danced, in reality Bogart was five inches shorter than Bergman, so he wore wooden blocks strapped to his shoes.

- The piano was painted pink so that it would look glowingly white on film.

- Although due for release in June 1943, Allied forces landed at Casablanca in November 1942 and it was rushed out just 18 days later in New York. Its general release in January coincided with the Casablanca Conference between the Allied Powers.

'Play it.'

Question: *What musical instrument did Dooley Wilson normally play?*

Chinatown
(1974)

Director: Roman Polanski

Length: 131 min   **Rating:** 15

Source: Screenplay by Robert Towne

J.J. Gittes	Jack Nicholson
Evelyn Mulwray	Faye Dunaway
Noah Cross	John Huston
Escobar	Perry Lopez
Yelburton	John Hillerman
Hollis Mulwray	Darrell Zwerling
Ida Sessions	Diane Ladd
Man with knife	Roman Polanski

This deliciously tortuous labyrinthine thriller is still quite simply one of the greatest movies of all time. Set in the 30s, Nicholson is the seedy private eye who gets pulled into a quicksand of corruption, murder and incest by *femme fatale* Dunaway. The witty script is so tortuous that it may need more than one viewing before you reckon you've nailed the plot down. But with such a wonderfully atmospheric film, who could complain about having to watch it again?

- Dunaway and Polanski did not get on. She found him a tyrant and he found her unnecessarily precious about her role, later saying: 'She was a gigantic pain in the ass.

She demonstrated certifiable proof of insanity.' It was a view with which Nicholson agreed, calling her 'certifiable'.

- To writer Towne's annoyance, Polanski rewrote the ending.

- Nicholson was dreading the scene where he gets washed down the storm drain. He came down so fast his shoes made huge dents in the mesh at the opening. Luckily, only the one take was needed.

> 'He passed away two weeks ago and he bought the land a week ago. That's unusual.'

Question: *How many Oscars was this film nominated for?*

Citizen Kane
(1941)

Director: Orson Welles

Length: 119 min   **Rating:** U

Source: Screenplay by Herman J. Mankiewicz & Orson Welles

Charles Foster Kane	Orson Welles
Jedediah Leland	Joseph Cotten
Susan Alexander	Dorothy Comingore
Mr. Bernstein	Everett Sloane
Boss J.W. 'Big Jim' Gettys	Ray Collins
Walter Parks Thatcher	George Coulouris
Raymond	Paul Stewart
Mary Kane	Agnes Moorehead
Kane's father	Harry Shannon
Emily Norton	Ruth Warrick

Widely regarded by critics as the best movie of all time, this quasi-documentary tale of an increasingly remote newspaper magnate was incredibly innovative. Deep focus photography meant you could see foreground and background at one and the same time. Despite the fantastic look to *Kane* and all Welles' tricks, the story itself drags and has been imitated many times. It's a cold film about a cold man.

• Despite Welles' self-publicity, much of the kudos for

the script should be placed at the door of Mankiewicz. According to writer Nunnally Johnson, Welles offered Mankiewicz $10,000 if he would take his name off the film. In the end, Welles had to be forced by the Screenwriters' Guild to credit his co-author.

- Welles worked his cast hard, with Cotten being forced to stay awake for 24 hours before his drunken scene.
- Unsurprisingly, newspaper tycoon William Randolph Hearst went to great lengths to prevent the film being made or distributed. Welles had to threaten to sue RKO before they would release it.

'I run a couple of newspapers. What do you do?'

Question: *What movie did Welles allegedly watch 40 times before embarking on this project?*

Dances With Wolves
(1990)

Director: Kevin Costner

Length: 179 min   **Rating:** 12

Source: Based on novel by Michael Blake

Lt. John J. Dunbar ....Kevin Costner
Stands With A Fist ....Mary McDonnell
Kicking Bird ....Graham Greene
Wind In His Hair ....Rodney A. Grant
Ten Bears ....Floyd Red Crow Westerman
Black Shawl ....Tantoo Cardinal
Timmons ....Robert Pastorelli
Lt. Elgin ....Charles Rocket

A remarkable directing debut from Costner. Despite its irritating and inaccurate Politically Correct stance, this story of a Civil War hero befriending and then joining the Sioux is a marvel. Proving that epics *can* still work, there's hardly a dull moment in a film which is fascinating, touching, shaming and even pretty funny in places. Despite the Western being such an old genre, the photography also dazzles the eye.

- So sure was Hollywood that Costner would come unstuck with this troubled production, which ran 30 days over schedule, that they nicknamed it *Kevin's Gate*, a reference to the disastrous *Heaven's Gate*.

- Revisionist it may be, but the 90s-style Indians, pacifist and green, certainly aren't historically accurate. According to one scholar: 'The Sioux massacred. They pillaged. They raped. They burned. They carried women and children into captivity. They tortured for entertainment. All this was their long-established custom, carried out, indeed, far more frequently against other Indian tribes than against whites.'

Question: *What can be seen around the dead wolf's neck?*

David Copperfield
(1935)

Brought To The Screen As Dickens Himself Would Wish It

Director: George Cukor

Length: 132 min   **Rating:** U

Source: Novel by Charles Dickens

Young David	Freddie Bartholomew
Adult David	Frank Lawton
Mr Micawber	W.C. Fields
Dan Peggotty	Lionel Barrymore
Peggotty	Jessie Ralph
Uriah Heep	Roland Young
Aunt Betsy	Edna May Oliver
Mr Murdstone	Basil Rathbone
Mrs Copperfield	Elizabeth Allan
Dora	Maureen O'Sullivan
Mrs Micawber	Jean Cadell

One of the very best screen versions of Dickens. It's a sumptuous production, reasonably honest to the source, and with an all-star cast pulling out all the stops. Fields gives the performance of his career. It was a deserved box office success.

• David O. Selznick and director Cukor had to fight Louis B. Mayer to stop him casting Jackie Cooper as the young Copperfield.

- Fields was initially very reluctant to do Micawber and wanted to relieve his anxiety by including a juggling routine!

- The studio originally cut the film to a more typical length, with Barrymore's role being dropped completely. But after viewing the movie Louis B. Mayer restored the majority of the cuts.

> 'Young friend, I counsel you. Annual income twenty pounds, annual expenditure nineteen pounds, result...happiness. Annual income twenty pounds, annual expenditure twenty-one pounds, result...misery.'

Question: *How did the director get Maureen O'Sullivan to cry?*

Dr Strangelove: Or How I Learned to Stop Worrying and Love the Bomb

(1963)

Director: Stanley Kubrick

Length: 93 min   **Rating:** PG

Source: Novel, *Red Alert* by Peter George

Dr Strangelove/Mandrake/Muffley	Peter Sellers
Gen. 'Buck' Turgidson	George C. Scott
Gen. Jack D. Ripper	Sterling Hayden
Col. 'Bat' Guano	Keenan Wynn
Maj. T.J. 'King' Kong	Slim Pickens
Ambassador de Sadesky	Peter Bull
Lt. Lothar Zogg	James Earl Jones
Miss Scott	Tracy Reed

War may be hell, but it can also be hellishly funny, as the Americans try to stop a renegade general triggering World War III. It's the high spot of Sellers' career as he plays a mad scientist, the American president and an RAF officer who just might be able to stop the ultimate madness. Despite the sadly dated effects of the bomber headed towards its target, it still manages to be both hilarious and chillingly believable.

- A custard-pie fight between the two sides in the War Room was filmed but not used.

- Some have pointed out that, as Henry Kissinger wasn't yet well known, Strangelove couldn't possibly be based on him. But Kubrick actually made a trip to Harvard to meet Kissinger while preparing for the movie.

- Sellers was due to play a fourth role, that of Major Kong. But he wasn't keen to do it and so faked an injury to his ankle, letting Pickens take the part.

> 'Gentlemen! You can't fight in here! This is the war room!'

Question: *Name the contemporary, more serious, film on the same subject.*

Double Indemnity
(1944)

Director: Billy Wilder

Length: 107 min   **Rating:** PG

Source: Magazine story by James M. Cain

Walter Neff	Fred MacMurray
Phyllis Dietrichson	Barbara Stanwyck
Barton Keyes	Edward G. Robinson
Mr Dietrichson	Tom Powers
Mr Jackson	Porter Hall
Lola Dietrichson	Jean Heather
Nino Zachette	Gig Young
Mr Norton	Richard Gaines
Sam Gorlopis	Fortunio Bonanova

Like a predatory insect, *femme fatale* Stanwyck ensnares insurance salesman MacMurray and then persuades him that with hubby out of the way, life would be so much more pleasant. MacMurray doesn't stop to think that some female insects eat their mates when their usefulness is over. This classic *film noir* never fades. The script sparkles with wit and fire and the photography is superb. But it's the performances that make it such a transport of delight. Stanwyck practically sets the screen on fire while the much underrated Robinson proves what a fine actor he could be when a role let him.

- The basis of the film was the true Snyder and Gray case of 1927.

- Many actors rejected the part of Neff, among them George Raft and Alan Ladd. MacMurray was for some time unwilling to take on a role so different to his usual clean-cut nice chap.

- The original ending, with MacMurray dying in the gas chamber, was felt too harrowing and the last 20 minutes were dropped. Wilder claims they were among the best scenes he ever made. Legend has it that the footage still exists.

> 'I wonder if I know what you mean.' – 'I wonder if you wonder.'

Question: *How many Oscars did this film win?*

Duck Soup

(1933)

Director: Leo McCarey

Length: 70 min   **Rating:** U

Source: Screenplay by Bert Kalmar, Harry Ruby, Arthur Sheekman & Nat Perrin

Rufus T. Firefly	Groucho Marx
Chicolini	Chico Marx
Brownie	Harpo Marx
Bob Rolland	Zeppo Marx
Mrs Teasdale	Margaret Dumont
Ambassador Trentino	Louis Calhern
Street vendor	Edgar Kennedy
Vera Marcal	Raquel Torres
Agitator	Leonid Kinsky
Prosecutor	Charles B. Middleton

The purest of all Marx Brothers' films is a masterpiece of zany humour. At the insistence of the wealthy Dumont, Groucho is installed as head of Freedonia and rapidly plunges the country into war. Although the plot's more haphazard than in their later MGM days, the gags flow thick and fast, there's some wonderful comic business and, best of all, that dreadful crooner Allan Jones is nowhere in sight.

- Mussolini was so offended by tinpot dictator Rufus T. Firefly that the film was banned in Italy, to the Marx Brothers' considerable delight. Their movies were already banned in Germany.

- Amazingly, the film was not a wow at the box office. As a result, Paramount dropped the Marx Brother's contract.

- This was Zeppo's last film.

> 'I could dance with you till the cows come home. On second thoughts, I'd rather dance with the cows till you came home.'

Question: *Who was the bald member of the cast?*

Easy Rider
(1969)

A Man Went Looking For America And Couldn't Find It Anywhere

Director: Dennis Hopper

Length: 94 min   **Rating:** 18

Source: Screenplay by Peter Fonda, Dennis Hopper & Terry Southern

Wyatt	Peter Fonda
Billy	Dennis Hopper
George Hanson	Jack Nicholson
Karen	Karen Black
Hippie leader	Robert Walker Jr.

In its day, a groundbreaking film, being the first to have drug dealers as heroes. Two bikers encounter various rednecks and dropouts as they head for New Orleans, only to learn that the American Dream is dead. It's interesting to see Hopper in youthful rebel mode, but Jack Nicholson gives the best performance. It's mainly of sociological interest these days.

• Hopper and Fonda sold the movie to Columbia for $355,000. It ended up taking more than $60m at the box office worldwide.

• The part of the lawyer was offered to Bruce Dern.

When he turned it down, Rip Torn took it but he and Hopper quarrelled. So the associate producer, an unknown part-time actor called Jack Nicholson, stepped in at the last moment.

- The scene in the cemetery with Fonda talking to the statue of the Madonna as if it's his mum affected him badly. His own mother killed herself when he was a kid, following which he tried to shoot himself. He begged Hopper to cut it, but Hopper refused.

- Although the film received an X certificate in Britain, it was the first movie to show drug taking and not be cut.

'You know, this used to be a hell of a good country. I can't understand what's wrong with it.'

Question: *What 'special effect' was an accident?*

E.T. The Extra-Terrestrial

(1982)

He Is Afraid. He Is Totally Alone. He Is 3 Million Light Years From Home

---

Director: Steven Spielberg

Length: 115 min   **Rating:** U

Source: Screenplay by Melissa Mathison

Mary . . . . .Dee Wallace
Elliott . . . . .Henry Thomas
Keys . . . . .Peter Coyote
Michael .Robert MacNaughton
Gertie . . . . .Drew Barrymore
Greg . . . . .K.C. Martel

Delightful, timeless family pic guaranteed to bring a lump to the throat and a tear to the eye, even if the effects look a little shaky a decade on. A bunch of kids adopt a wacky little alien and then fight off the adults when he wants to return home. Funny, fascinating and occasionally frightening, this splendidly-directed film (almost all shot from a child's-eye view) deservedly became the most successful of all time, grossing over $700m worldwide. Full marks to Spielberg, too, for never spoiling it by giving us a sequel.

• Both Disney and Universal passed on the film, after tests showed the public wouldn't be interested. The

film took more in its opening weekend alone than the $10.5m it cost to make.

- The drunk scene was done by legless schoolboy Matthew de Merrit, walking on his hands inside the costume.

- Sweden wouldn't allow children under 12 to see the movie because it showed parents reprimanding their children.

- M&M refused permission to use their sweets in the film so E.T. followed a trail of Reese's Pieces instead. Sales promptly doubled.

'E.T. phone home.'

Question: *How was E.T.'s face designed?*

Fantasia

(1940)

Fantasia will Amaze-Ya

Director: Ben Sharpsteen

Length: 120 min   **Rating:** U

Source: Screenplay by various writers

Narrator ....Deems Taylor
Conductor ....Leopold Stokowski

This project, merging art and popular culture by accompanying assorted pieces of classical music with animated pictures, was dear to Walt's heart. Despite its apparent popularity, the accompanying visual effects sometimes fail to quite hit their targets. The dancing hippos and lascivious crocodiles are great fun, as is Mickey's Sorcerer's Apprentice, although it's easy to see why the Pastoral Symphony with its scantily-clad nymphs caused consternation at the time. Night on Bald Mountain is one of the best conceived segments and still has a good shiver quotient, even if the Shubert makes for a rather dull ending. Stokowski's conducting is fabulous, and what other film allows the audience to meet the soundtrack?

- It was a financial disaster on first release. Cinemas needed the expensive 'Fantasound' multi-speaker system to do it justice. However, it became a constant source of revenue in later years, helped by stories that it took on a whole new light under the influence of drugs.

- For its 50th birthday, it was released with a re-recorded Dolby stereo soundtrack. Only then was it discovered that for the previous 40 years, the music had been two frames out of synch with the pictures.

- By claiming that the videos were only going to be available to buy for a limited period in the 90s, it became a best-selling title in Britain.

> 'This will *make* Beethoven'. [Walt Disney]

Question: *Who provided the voice of Mickey Mouse?*

42nd Street

(1933)

Director: Lloyd Bacon

Length: 89 min

Source: Novel by Bradford Ropes

Julian Marsh	Warner Baxter
Peggy Sawyer	Ruby Keeler
Dorothy Brock	Bebe Daniels
Pat Denning	George Brent
Lorraine Fleming	Una Merkel
Abner Dillon	Guy Kibbee
Billy Lawler	Dick Powell
Anytime Annie	Ginger Rogers
MacElroy	Allen Jenkins
Barry	Ned Sparks

The first of the all-wisecracking, all-singing, all-dancing Warner Bros. backstage musicals is packed with original lines and situations that only later became clichés. Yet it still all seems wonderfully fresh as the boys and girls of the chorus prepare for their big opening night. Audiences were understandably knocked over by choreographer Busby Berkeley's production numbers. Among the songs are 'I'm Young and Healthy', 'Shuffle Off to Buffalo' and 'You're Getting to be a Habit With Me'. Pure joy.

- The first real movie musical. Daryl F. Zanuck came up with the idea for an antidote to the Depression in the form of a fantasy musical.

- Busby Berkeley got the taste for choreography as a drill master in World War One. Although he had worked on over 20 Broadway musicals, this was his first major Hollywood movie.

- Berkeley apparently auditioned 5,000 prospective chorus girls, picking out only those he thought the prettiest. They were all put on a strict diet and fitness regime and even their sleeping times were supervised.

'Go out there and be so swell you'll make me hate you.'

Question: *How many musicals did Powell and Keeler make together?*

Frankenstein

(1931)

To Have Seen It Is To Wear A Badge Of Courage!

Director: James Whale

Length: 71 min   **Rating:** PG

Source: Novel by Mary Shelley and play by Peggy Webling

Henry Frankenstein ....Colin Clive
Elizabeth ....Mae Clarke
The Monster ....Boris Karloff
Victor Moritz ....John Boles
Dr Waldman ....Edward Van Sloan
Fritz, the dwarf ....Dwight Frye
Baron Frankenstein ....Frederick Kerr
Herr Vogel, the Burgomaster ......Lionel Belmore

This most famous of all horror films may creak a little in the joints but it's still immensely watchable, if not particularly scary any more. The story of the scientist creating life from dead tissue is always fascinating, of course, but this has the additional benefit of beautiful gothic sets and a great-looking creature that inspires sympathy as well as fear. There were umpteen sequels and remakes, the best being *The Bride of Frankenstein* and *Young Frankenstein*.

• It took four hours for Karloff to be made up as the

monster each day. A brace kept his spine rigid and he wore leg braces to give him that strange gait. It was pretty tough for Karloff as they were filming in the middle of summer. He sweated so much, the monster's head kept melting and needed constant repairs.

- The filmmakers wanted to keep the look of *Frankenstein* secret so Karloff was hidden under a sheet when he went from the make-up room to the set.

- Horror films were still a rarity so the studio added a warning prologue and hired nurses to be on hand in the lobby of many cinemas.

'It's alive! It's alive!'

Question: *Why did Bela Lugosi refused to play the monster?*

The French Connection
(1971)

Doyle Is Bad News...But A Good Cop

Director: William Friedkin

Length: 104 min   **Rating:** 18

Source: Novel by Robin Moore

Jimmy 'Popeye' Doyle	Gene Hackman
Alain Charnier	Fernando Rey
Buddy Russo	Roy Scheider
Sal Boca	Tony Lo Bianco
Pierre Nicoli	Marcel Bozzuffi
Devereaux	Frederic De Pasquale

A tough, unconventional New York cop obsessively tracks down a drugs shipment. A revelation at the time for blurring the distinctions between the police and the crooks, for its use of locations and for its near-documentary style, it is most memorable for the stunning scenes where Hackman chases a subway train in a car. It's a shame it's so hard to hear what the characters are saying at times, especially as this naturalist sound was then copied by so many other movies.

- The novel and film were based on real narcotics agents Eddie 'Popeye' Egan and Sonny Grosso who solved a major case involving a New York drug syndicate in

1961. However the Police didn't like the way they
came across in the film and Egan, who had been a cop
for 16 years and made over 8000 arrests, was sacked
just seven hours before he was due to retire. As a result,
he didn't qualify for his pension. He received only
$240 from the movie.

- Hackman did the driving in the great chase himself, at
speeds of up to 90 miles per hour. It took five weeks to
film. Although restricting some of the side routes, the
filmmakers weren't able to stop the traffic on the route
Hackman takes. Those cars he's dodging are filled with
ordinary unsuspecting John Does.

'Alright, Popeye's here!'

Question: *What character does the real-life 'Popeye' play?*

From Here to Eternity

(1953)

The Boldest Book Of Our Time, Honestly, Fearlessly On The Screen

---

Director: Fred Zinnemann

Length: 118 min   **Rating:** PG

Source: Novel by James Jones

Sgt. Milton A. Warden	Burt Lancaster
Karen Holmes	Deborah Kerr
Pte. Robert E. Lee Prewitt	Montgomery Clift
Angelo Maggio	Frank Sinatra
Alma Lorene	Donna Reed
Sgt. 'Fatso' Judson	Ernest Borgnine
Capt. Dana Holmes	Philip Ober
Sgt. Leva	Mickey Shaughnessy
Cpl. Buckley	Jack Warden
Mazzioli	Harry Bellaver

Life in an army barracks in Hawaii in the days leading up to the Japanese attack on Pearl Harbor. Much to the author's fury, the film ended up as a much toned down version of the massive novel. Nevertheless, it remains a powerful portrayal of service life before World War Two. It includes the famous roll in the surf with Kerr and Lancaster.

- Although the US Navy banned the film because it was 'derogatory to a sister service', the army allowed it to be shown at any of its bases around the world.

- Sinatra's career was in a bad way, with singing temporarily impossible because of a throat problem, and he had to beg to play the part after Eli Wallach dropped out. He did it for just $8,000, but it resuscitated his career.

- Clift learnt to play the bugle for his part but the bugle calls were actually dubbed for the film.

> 'I love the Army. A man loves a thing, that doesn't mean it's got to love him back.'

Question: *Who was originally to have played Kerr's part?*

Gaslight
(1940)

Director: Thorold Dickinson

Length: 88 min

Source: Play by Patrick Hamilton

Paul Mallen	Anton Walbrook
Bella Mallen	Diana Wynyard
Rough	Frank Pettingell
Nancy	Cathleen Cordell
Ullswater	Robert Newton

Is a new bride having hallucinations, or is her husband trying to unsettle her mind? This superb psychological chiller still delivers the goods even today, suffused as it is with a nicely creepy atmosphere and beautifully understated performances. It was also known in America as *Angel Street*. The MGM remake in 1944 with Charles Boyer and Ingrid Bergman is lushly entertaining, but not as scary as the original. Under the polished direction of Dickinson, this is one of the most stylish British films to be made before the war.

• Columbia purchased the rights to the film in 1941, intending an American re-make starring Irene Dunne. Then MGM bought it as a vehicle for Heddy Lamaar.

Question: *How did Ingrid Bergman get the lead in the 1944 production?*

The General
(1926)

Director: Buster Keaton & Clyde Bruckman
Length: 88 min
Source: Book, *The Great Locomotive Chase* by William Pittenger

Johnnie Gray	Buster Keaton
Annabelle Lee	Marion Mack
Capt. Anderson	Glen Cavender
Union Gen. Thatcher	Jim Farley

When a group of Union soldiers hijack a Confederate locomotive, its driver is determined to get it back. This now comes across as Buster Keaton's finest film. Although it may not be as anarchic as some of his films, it is beautifully paced with great sight gags.

- The film was based on a true incident, although the episode actually ended with the hijackers being caught and several executed.
- Keaton had a pair of original locomotives restored for the movie. However, his wish that they be run on wood rather than coal caused a forest fire during production.
- The scene with the bridge collapsing with the engine on it was, according to Kevin Brownlow, the single most expensive shot in silent film history.

Question: *What was the fate of the engine at the bottom of the ravine?*

The Godfather

(1972)

Director: Francis Ford Coppola
Length: 175 min   **Rating:** 18
Source: Novel by Mario Puzo

Don Vito Corleone	Marlon Brando
Michael Corleone	Al Pacino
Sonny Corleone	James Caan
Clemenza	Richard Castellano
Tom Hagen	Robert Duvall
McCluskey	Sterling Hayden
Kay Adams	Diane Keaton
Connie Rizzi	Talia Shire
Jack Woltz	John Marley
Barzini	Richard Conte

The trials and tribulations of running a Family business in the face of cut-throat opposition. This epic Mafia saga is a powerful and entertaining piece of storytelling which was a well-deserved box office smash. An invitation to watch this is an offer you won't be able to refuse, even if understanding Brando can be something of a trial at times. It was followed by *The Godfather Part II* in 1974 and *Part III* in 1990.

• Enthusiasm for a picture about the Mafia wasn't exactly rampant at Paramount. Peter Yates and

Arthur Penn were offered the chance to direct it before Coppola.

- As well as stuffing his mouth with cotton wool, Brando plugged his ears throughout filming, the idea being that he would have to concentrate harder when others were talking.

- After meeting real-life Godfather Anthony Columbo, the film-makers agreed that the words 'Mafia' or 'Cosa Nostra' not be mentioned at any point.

- The horse's head in the bed is not a prop, but a real head.

'I'm gonna make him an offer he can't refuse.'

Question: *Who is the baby in the baptism scene?*

Goldfinger
(1964)

Director: Guy Hamilton

Length: 112 min   **Rating:** PG

Source: Novel by Ian Fleming

James Bond	Sean Connery
Pussy Galore	Honor Blackman
Auric Goldfinger	Gert Frobe
Jill Masterson	Shirley Eaton
Oddjob	Harold Sakata
'M'	Bernard Lee
Miss Moneypenny	Lois Maxwell
'Q'	Desmond Llewelyn
Tilly Masterson	Tania Mallett
Solo	Martin Benson
Felix Leiter	Cec Linder

The third in the Bond series still maintained a high standard, with Bond trying to stop an attack on the gold supply at Fort Knox. It's packed full of memorable moments, with Oddjob and his lethal bowler hat, the gold-painted death of Shirley Eaton and a laser beam that nearly brings tears to Bond's eyes and it's all topped off with a great theme song. What more could any Bond fan want?

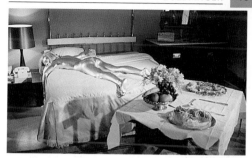

- Costing just under $3m, the film made $45m around the world.

- The producers were well aware how cheeky Blackman's character's name was and were fully prepare to have to redub it to Kitty if the censors asked them to.

- Ian Fleming died a fortnight before *Goldfinger* opened

- The Aston Martin DB6 was sold at auction in 1986 for $275,000, the most ever for a movie prop.

- The Queen Mother declared this the best film she had ever seen.

> 'Do you expect me to talk?' – 'No, Mr. Bond. I expect you to die.'

Question: *Where were the Fort Knox scenes filmed?*

Gone with the Wind
(1939)

Director: Victor Fleming, George Cukor & Sam Wood

Length: 220 min   **Rating:** PG

Source: Novel by Margaret Mitchell

Rhett Butler . . . . .Clark Gable
Scarlett O'Hara . . . . .Vivien Leigh
Ashley Wilkes .Leslie Howard
Melanie Hamilton . . . . .Olivia De Havilland
Gerald O'Hara .Thomas Mitchell
Ellen O'Hara . . . . .Barbara O'Neil
Mammy . . . . .Hattie McDaniel
Prissy . . . . .Butterfly McQueen
Aunt 'Pittypat' Hamilton . . . . . . .Laura Hope Crews
Stuart Tarleton .George Reeves
Dr Meade . . . . .Harry Davenport

The ultimate soap opera is a one-off the like of which
we shall never see again. Leigh was surely the right
choice for feisty, selfish Scarlett O'Hara, around whom
this tale of love and betrayal at the time of the American
Civil War revolves. With the possible exception of the
miscast Leslie Howard, every single actor does their bit.
Despite its running time, there are surprisingly few flat
patches and the tedium is soon dispelled when the
compelling story sweeps us along again.

- Although Gable was the only serious choice for Rhett, a nationwide talent competition was launched to find Scarlett, providing excellent advance publicity.

- Filming began with George Cukor at the helm but Gable was said to be unhappy with the 'woman's director' and he was replaced with Victor Fleming, who was taken off *The Wizard of Oz*. When he had a nervous breakdown, Sam Wood took over his duties for a time.

- Hattie McDaniel was the first black actor to win an Oscar.

- Producer, Selznick had to pay a fine of $5,000 for using the word 'damn'.

> 'Frankly, my dear, I don't give a damn!'

Question: *Who was the guest of honour at the film's 50th anniversary bash?*

GoodFellas
(1990)

Director: Martin Scorsese
Length: 146 min   **Rating:** 18
Source: Book *Wiseguy* by Nicholas Pileggi

James Conway ....Robert De Niro
Henry Hill ....Ray Liotta
Tommy DeVito ....Joe Pesci
Karen Hill ....Lorraine Bracco
Paul Cicero ....Paul Sorvino
Frenchy ....Mike Starr
Billy Batts ....Frank Vincent
Morris Kessler ....Chuck Low
Tommy's mother ....Catherine Scorsese

A dazzlingly brilliant depiction of the allure and often sad reality of life within the Mafia, centring around the criminal career of Liotta. Although violent, direction, script, photography and performances are all out of the top drawer. One expects great things of Pesci and De Niro, but Liotta and Bracco, as the mistreated wife turned-on by the violence, are also both superb.

• Based on the real-life story of gangster Henry Hill, now in the Witness Protection Plan. Hill's response to the film was: 'That's really the way it was. It's all true.'

• According to the Entertainment Research Group, the

F-word appears 246 times. There's an obscenity on average every 30 seconds, probably the current record.

- Although often seen briefly in his films, Scorsese's mother has a proper part this time as Pesci's screen mom, while Charles Scorsese is Vinnie.

- Look out for Samuel L. Jackson in a small role as 'Stacks Edwards'.

'As far back as I can remember, I've always wanted to be a gangster. To me, being a gangster was better than being President of the United States. You were treated like a film star.'

Question: *What film held the previous record for obscenities?*

The Graduate
(1967)

This is Benjamin. He's A Little Worried About His Future!

Director: Mike Nichols

Length: 105 min   **Rating:** 15

Source: Novel by Charles Webb

Mrs Robinson	Anne Bancroft
Ben Braddock	Dustin Hoffman
Elaine Robinson	Katharine Ross
Mr Braddock	William Daniels
Mr Robinson	Murray Hamilton
Mrs Braddock	Elizabeth Wilson
Mr McCleery	Norman Fell
Mrs Singleman	Alice Ghostley
Room clerk	Buck Henry
Miss de Witt	Marion Lorne

His college days over, a young graduate tries to resist the universal pressures to decide what he should do with his life. He is seduced by his parents' best friend, while falling in love with her daughter. Hoffman has never been funnier while Bancroft is so electrifyingly sexy that it is impossible to understand why Ben would choose the insipid Elaine over her.

- Director Nichols introduced many new camera techniques that had been used in adverts but not in commercial cinema.

- Another innovation was to use popular songs on the soundtrack that were not related to what was happening on screen. Simon and Garfunkel's 'The Sound of Silence' had been at the top of the charts in 1966. 'Mrs. Robinson' went to Number One in 1968.

- After filming was over, Hoffman went back onto the dole, not expecting the film to be a success.

'Do you find me undesirable?' – 'Oh no, Mrs. Robinson. I think...I think you're the most attractive of all my parents' friends. I mean that.'

Question: *Who was first choice for the part of Ben?*

The Grapes of Wrath
(1940)

Director: John Ford

Length: 129 min   **Rating:** PG

Source: Novel by John Steinbeck

Tom Joad	Henry Fonda
Ma Joad	Jane Darwell
Casey	John Carradine
Grampa Joad	Charley Grapewin
Rosaharn	Dorris Bowden
Pa Joad	Russell Simpson
Muley	John Qualen
Connie	Eddie Quillan
Al	O.Z. Whitehead
Grandma Joad	Zeffie Tilbury
Guardian	Grant Mitchell
Winfield	Darryl Hickman

A family of poor farmers, under pressure from big business interests that want machines to cultivate the land, abandon their dust-bowl farm and head off to California in search of a better life. But they aren't the only ones. Not just one of the finest social dramas but one of the most heart-rending films of all time.

- Before proceeding with the production, Fox head Darryl Zanuck had teams of investigators head for the

migrant camps to see if the book told the truth about the situation. If anything, came back the reports, the novel was too optimistic.

- Ford tried to keep the film as fresh as possible by getting as many scenes as he could in the can the first time.

- As bankers to the production company, the directors of Chase National Bank will have profited from the film, even though it was also one of those which controlled the land companies that pushed people like the Joads off their land.

'I jus' trying to get on without shovin' anybody, that's all.'

Question: *Why was this film banned in Russia?*

A Hard Day's Night
(1964)

Director: Richard Lester

Length: 85 min   **Rating:** U

Source: Screenplay by Alun Owen

John	John Lennon
Paul	Paul McCartney
George	George Harrison
Ringo	Ringo Starr
Grandfather	Wilfrid Brambell
Norm	Norman Rossington
Shake	John Junkin
TV director	Victor Spinetti
Police Inspector	Deryck Guyler
Millie	Anna Quayle

This movie purports to show us a day and a half in the company of a popular musical singing group of the 60s, with life complicated by the rascally grandfather of one of the band members. This innovative movie, utilizing lots of techniques popular in the commercials' world, would have been funny whoever starred in it. As it features The Beatles just after they had made it, it is not only hilarious, but absolutely riveting. The music, it hardly needs to be said, is out of this world.

- Filmed in just six and a half weeks, the budget was only £180,000, with United Artists more interested in the soundtrack album than they were in the movie.

- With Beatlemania at its height, most of the filming outside had to be got in the can in the first or second take before a mob of fans appeared.

- Although it has the feel of an ad-libbed movie, it was only the press conference that was improvised.

- George Harrison met future wife Patti Boyd during the movie. When John, Paul and George are in the dining car, she is the blonde one of the two schoolgirls.

> 'He's a *clean* old man.'

Question: *Who came up with the unusual title?*

Henry V
(1944)

Director: Laurence Olivier

Length: 137 min   **Rating:** U

Source: Play by William Shakespeare

King Henry V	Laurence Olivier
Ancient Pistol	Robert Newton
Chorus	Leslie Banks
Princess Katherine	Renée Asherson
Fluellen	Esmond Knight
Contable of France	Leo Genn
Archbishop of Canterbury	Felix Aylmer
Mountjoy	Ralph Truman
King Charles VI of France	Harcourt Williams
Sir John Falstaff	George Robey

This best of all screen versions of his plays cleverly starts as a filmed piece of theatre, gradually becomes more realistic, and then comes round full circle to end as a stage play again. Olivier gives one of his greatest performances. Even in peacetime, it can get the patriotic blood racing. At the time, it must have been an amazing tonic to embattled Britons.

• Olivier only agreed to direct the movie when William Wyler, Terence Young and Carol Reed turned the project down.

- Olivier's wife Vivien Leigh couldn't get permission from producer, Selznick, to leave Hollywood to play Queen Katherine. Asherson was chosen in large part because she was a similar size to Leigh and the costumes had already been made.

- Filmed in neutral Ireland, the production used the only Technicolor camera in the British Isles. Many of the extras were local farmers and soldiers from Enniskerry.

- Olivier's lip was split when a horse hit the camera, scarring him for life.

'Norman bastards.'

Question: *Can you identify who plays 'The Boy' (you have to keep your eyes peeled)?*

High Noon
(1952)

**When These Hands Stand Straight Up...
The Excitement Starts**

Director: Fred Zinnemann

Length: 85 min   **Rating:** U

Source: Story, *The Tin Star* by John W. Cunningham

Will Kane	Gary Cooper
Amy Kane	Grace Kelly
Jonas Henderson	Thomas Mitchell
Harvey Pell	Lloyd Bridges
Helen Ramirez	Katy Jurado
Percy Mettrick	Otto Kruger
Martin Howe	Lon Chaney Jr.
William Fuller	Harry Morgan
Cooper	Harry Shannon
Jack Colby	Lee Van Cleef

The story of Gary Cooper standing alone to defend Hadleyville from four gunmen is an old story. What has kept this film a classic is Zinnemann's brisk pace (one of those rare films set in 'real time') and the elimination of a lot of tiresome background characterisation. Grace Kelly had yet to be thawed out by Hitchcock, but the cast is otherwise excellent, and the theme tune and rhythmic editing help immeasurably.

- 'Real time' filming was a nightmare for the continuity girl who had to make sure that the clocks were always properly set. The film's running time of 85 minutes actually covers 90 minutes.

- When producer Stanley Kramer realized that the movie was too slow, he inserted lots of closeups of Cooper's tired face and repeated shots of clocks counting the minutes to noon.

- After the first preview fell flat, Kramer asked composer Dmitri Tiomkin to come up with a song. 'Do Not Forsake Me, Oh My Darling' won an Oscar.

> 'It's no good. I've got to go back. They're making me run. I've never run from anyone before.'

Question: *Why did writer Carl Foreman leave the US?*

In the Heat of the Night
(1967)

Director: Norman Jewison

Length: 109 min   **Rating:** 15

Source: Novel by John Ball

Virgil Tibbs	Sidney Poitier
Bill Gillespie	Rod Steiger
Deputy Sam Wood	Warren Oates
Delores Purdy	Quentin Dean
Purdy	James Patterson
Webb Schubert	William Schallert
Mrs Leslie Colbert	Lee Grant
Eric Endicott	Larry Gates
Mama Baleba	Beah Richards
Harvey Oberst	Scott Wilson

A Southern sheriff is astounded to find a black detective sent along to help him solve a murder case. As the two work together, however, they develop a mutual respect and affection. Steiger and Poitier are both splendid, with Steiger particularly believable as the man having to reconsider lifelong beliefs. The two combine to made this a superb thriller. Poitier would later go on to play the same role in *They Call Me* Mister *Tibbs* and *The Organization*.

- Steiger stayed in character even when the cameras weren't rolling and was never without gum in his mouth.

- When director Jewison said he wasn't tubby enough, Steiger was only too delighted to pig himself on desserts. 'I gladly sacrificed myself to art. If I had only two pieces of pecan pie, they went mad. So I gorged myself.'

- Norman Jewison avoided sentimentality and racial cliché, and the film shocked many by winning an Oscar for Best Film, despite stiff competition.

'They call me *Mr.* Tibbs.'

Question: *Where was the movie filmed?*

Intolerance
(1916)

Director: D.W. Griffith
Length: 175 min
Source: Screenplay by D.W. Griffith

The Woman Who Rocks the Cradle .....Lillian Gish
The Boy ....Robert Harron
The Dear One ....Mae Marsh
Girl from the Mountains ......Constance Talmadge
The Bride of Cana ....Bessie Love
Prosper Latour ....Eugene Pallette
Pharisee (and others) ....Erich von Stroheim

Few epics come bigger than this. Four narratives – the fall of Babylon, the St Bartholomew's Day Massacre, the life of Christ and a modern-day execution – are interwoven to contrast intolerance across the ages. The sentiments are sometimes Victorian, but on a big screen with music it is amazing how well this film, called by some the most important movie ever made, still works.

- Although film buffs point out many firsts for the film, such as the giant crane used for the Babylon sequence, just as important was Griffith's invention to make Princess Beloved's eyes more exciting: false eyelashes.

- Griffith hired some prostitutes to appear naked at the orgiastic Belshazar's Feast. When the movie was re-

released in 1942, New Yorks' censors insisted on them being struck out.

- Because of this scene, which Griffith didn't want cut out, the film was not submitted to the BBFC in Britain. As a result, the film had a limited release here.

- *Intolerance* was not a success with audiences. After initial interest, takings fell off, its final plea for tolerance and peace being out of tune with a nation gearing up for war.

'The only film fugue'

Question: *Why did the fire brigade turn up?*

Invasion of the Body Snatchers

(1956)

There Was Nothing To Hold On To – Except Each Other

Director: Don Siegel

Length: 80 min   **Rating**: PG

Source: Novel, *The Body Snatchers* by Jack Finney

Dr Miles Bennel	Kevin McCarthy
Becky Driscoll	Dana Wynter
Dr Dan Kauffman	Larry Gates
Jack	King Donovan
Theodora	Carolyn Jones
Wilma Lentz	Virginia Christine
Nick Grivett	Ralph Dumke
Uncle Ira	Tom Fadden
Psychiatrist	Whit Bissell
Gas man	Sam Peckinpah

A doctor discovers aliens are doing away with his fellow townspeople, replacing them with inhuman replicas. Despite its low budget, this is one of the great paranoia movies, chilling in concept and terrifyingly plausible in execution. A 76-minute version, without the prologue and epilogue, is better than the original release.

- The studio bosses were so frightened when they saw the film that they insisted on explanatory bookends at the start and end of the film, just in case people though it was all real.

- Although it was ignored by the critics, it became a big hit with the public.

- Sam Peckinpah appears as a meter reader. He was down on his luck, so Siegel gave the role to him out of friendship.

> 'While you're asleep, they'll absorb your mind, your memories, and you'll be reborn into an untroubled world.'

Question: *What was the working title of this film?*

The Invisible Man
(1933)

Director: James Whale

Length: 71 min

Source: Novel by H.G. Wells

Jack Griffin	Claude Rains
Flora Cranley	Gloria Stuart
Dr Kemp	William Harrigan
Dr Cranley	Henry Travers
Mrs. Hall	Una O'Connor
Chief of Detectives	Dudley Digges
Mr Hall	Forrester Harvey
Jaffers	E.E. Clive

A scientist finds a way to make himself invisible but he gets progressively loopier as well, until he becomes a dangerous menace. Some of the performances now seem a little melodramatic but, amazingly, most of the special effects look fine even today while the jokey tone makes it all good fun. There were umpteen sequels and imitators, among them *The Invisible Man Returns*, *The Invisible Woman*, *Abbott and Costello Meet the Invisible Man*, as well as the more recent *Memoirs of an Invisible Man*.

- Rains, completely invisible, escapes from the burning barn and dashes across the snow. The reason he's invisible is that he is totally naked. Yet in one of the greatest of all cinema gaffes, he leaves, not footprints for the police to follow in the snow, but *shoeprints*!

- Would a British police station really have the words 'Police Department' on the door?

- This was Claude Rains' cinema debut, although moviegoers didn't get to see much of him.

> 'We'll start with a reign of terror, a few murders here and there. Murders of great men, murders of little men. Just to show we make no distinction.'

Question: *Why did Boris Karloff refuse the lead?*

It's a Wonderful Life
(1946)

Director: Frank Capra

Length: 129 min   **Rating:** U

Source: Story, *The Greatest Gift* by Philip Van Doren Stern

George Bailey . . . . .James Stewart
Mary Hatch . . . . .Donna Reed
Mr Potter . . . . .Lionel Barrymore
Clarence Oddbody . . . . .Henry Travers
Uncle Billy . . . . .Thomas Mitchell
Mrs. Bailey . . . . .Beulah Bondi
Ernie . . . . .Frank Faylen
Bert . . . . .Ward Bond
Violet Bick . . . . .Gloria Grahame
Mr Gower . . . . .H.B. Warner

An all-round nice guy finds himself so beset by troubles that he toys with the idea of killing himself, only to have an angel appear to show him what life in Bedford Falls would be like without him. This is one of the loveliest, kindliest, happiest and most emotional films ever made. There are few movies that can coax the tears out every time on cue like this one. By the end, you're so glad to be alive, you just want to go round and hug everyone you meet.

- Van Doren Stern sent the story out to his friends one year on his Christmas cards and got such a good response that it was published.

- Both Stewart and Capra had been in the services and had had no offers of work during the months since they had left. Stewart remained grateful to Capra for the job that got him back into movies for the rest of his life.

- The film was colourised, even though Capra fought hard to prevent it happening.

> 'Get me back. I don't care what happens to me. Get me back to my wife and kids. Help me, Clarence. Please! Please! I wanna live again. I wanna live again. I wanna live again. Please, God, let me live again!'

Question: *How many Oscars did the film win?*

Jaws
(1975)

She Was The First

Director: Steven Spielberg

Length: 124 min   **Rating:** PG

Source: Novel by Peter Benchley

Martin Brody	Roy Scheider
Capt. Quint	Robert Shaw
Matt Hooper	Richard Dreyfuss
Ellen Brody	Lorraine Gary
Mayor Vaughan	Murray Hamilton
Meadows	Carl Gottlieb
Deputy Hendricks	Jeffrey C. Kramer
Chrissie Watkins	Susan Backlinie
Cassidy	Jonathan Filley
Interviewer	Peter Benchley

Okay, okay. So the shark looks just a little rubbery 20 years on. But with that one caveat, this tale of a Great White treating holiday time at a New England resort as an eat-all-you-can buffet is still riveting stuff. That's due, in the main, to beautifully assured direction from a 27-year-old Spielberg and a trio of splendid performances from Scheider, Shaw and Dreyfuss. Scheider hung around for the limp sequel, but sensibly opted out of the further two dreadful *Jaws* films.

- The opening shark attack was simulated by having five guys pulling on ropes attached to the girl in the water. They were so enthusiastic, they broke two of her ribs.

- The scene in which the shark sinks the *Orca* happened but was not planned. Fortunately, the film was recovered by divers and immediately sluiced down and developed.

- The American release was deliberately delayed until the beginning of the summer beach season.

- This was the first big merchandized movie, with *Jaws* T-shirts, bikinis, socks, beach towels, lunch boxes, tote bags, blow-up toys, posters and plastic fins.

'You're gonna need a bigger boat.'

Question: *How many sharks were used in the film?*

Kind Hearts and Coronets
(1949)

Director: Robert Hamer

Length: 105 min   **Rating:** U

Source: Novel, *Israel Rank* by Roy Horniman

Louis Mazzini	Dennis Price
Edith D'Ascoyne	Valerie Hobson
Sibella	Joan Greenwood
The Duke/ The Banker/	
The Parson/ The General/	
The Admiral/ Young Ascoyne	
D'Ascoyne/ Young Henry/	
Lady Agatha	Alec Guinness
Mama	Audrey Fildes
Hangman	Miles Malleson
Prison Governor	Clive Morton
Lionel	John Penrose
Lord High Steward	Hugh Griffith
Reporter	Arthur Lowe

Hating those disdainful relatives that stand between him and the dukedom he considers rightfully his, a young man increases his chance of inheritance by doing away with those nearer the title. In this splendid black comedy, Guinness outdoes himself playing eight of the D'Ascoynes, Price is suitably cold-blooded and Greenwood is incredibly sexy. The wonderfully witty and literate script keeps the film fresh no matter how many times you watch it.

- The ending was originally much vaguer and thus more satisfying. Then word came that the American censors would not allow the movie to be released because crime could not be seen to pay, so the final scene had to be tacked on.

- For the scene with the balloon, a Belgian balloonist was brought in. Things didn't go according to plan, however, and the chap couldn't bring the balloon down to earth again for 50 miles.

'It is so difficult to make a neat job of killing people with whom one is not on friendly terms.'

Question: *How many parts was Guinness meant to play?*

King Kong
(1933)

The Eighth Wonder Of The World

Director: Merian C. Cooper & Ernest B. Schoedsack

Length: 100 min   **Rating:** PG

Source: Story by Edgar Wallace

Ann Darrow	Fay Wray
Carl Denham	Robert Armstrong
John Driscoll	Bruce Cabot
Capt. Englehorn	Frank Reicher
Charles Weston	Sam Hardy
Native chief	Noble Johnson
2nd mate Briggs	James Flavin
Socrates	Paul Porcasi

A giant ape is brought back to New York by an expedition to be exhibited but it escapes and creates havoc. Like so many movies in which enormous effort was expended on the effects, the story isn't always strong enough to carry the strain. The effects themselves have held up surprisingly well considering how innovative they then were and there are many delights along the way, not least the less-than-subtle sexual subtext of this Beauty and the Beast tale.

- King Kong is mainly an 18-inch model, filmed by taking a frame of film, moving the model's limbs and eyes imperceptibly, then filming another frame, and so on. For some shots, as where Wray is in Kong's paw, large models were built.

- Although the native language was pure gibberish, the film couldn't get past the censors until an English translation was provided for them.

- Cooper and Schoedsack appear at the end as the Flight Commander and his observer delivering the death blow to Kong. They thought it was only fitting that they killed their own creation.

> 'Oh, no, it wasn't the airplanes. It was beauty killed the beast.' [Last line]

Question: *Who's favourite movie was this?*

The Last Picture Show
(1971)

Director: Peter Bogdanovich

Length: 118 min   **Rating:** U

Source: Novel by Larry McMurtry

Sonny Crawford	Timothy Bottoms
Duane Jackson	Jeff Bridges
Jacy Farrow	Cybill Shepherd
Sam the Lion	Ben Johnson
Ruth Popper	Cloris Leachman
Lois Farrow	Ellen Burstyn
Genevieve	Eileen Brennan
Abilene	Clu Gulager
Charlene Duggs	Sharon Taggart
Bill	Sam Bottoms

A beautiful slice-of-life look centring on the lives of assorted youngsters in a fading Midwestern American town. Although ultimately rather bleak, it is a beautifully observed piece of nostalgia. Some grumble that Bogdanovich's style is terribly derivative but, at a time when directors were cramming any old gimmick into their movies in a desperate attempt to liven things up, it now comes as a relief to see something from that period that isn't so showy.

- When Ben Johnson originally refused to do the film, Bogdanovich told him that he would win an Oscar if he did it. Leachman claims he said the same to her, claiming that anyone playing her part would win one.

- Bogdanovich was right. Johnson did win an Oscar for Best Supporting Actor; and Leachman won Best Supporting Actress. The film was nominated for eight Academy Awards in total.

- The director was an admirer of the styles of Ford and Hawks, and was hailed at the time as the new Orson Welles.

Question: *What movies are playing at the cinema?*

The Lavender Hill Mob
(1951)

Director: Charles Crichton

Length: 82 min   **Rating:** U

Source: Screenplay by T.E.B. Clarke

Henry Holland	Alec Guinness
Pendlebury	Stanley Holloway
Lackery	Sidney James
Shorty	Alfie Bass
Mrs Chalk	Marjorie Fielding
Miss Evesham	Edie Martin
Farrow	John Gregson
Godwin	Gibb McLaughlin
Chiquita	Audrey Hepburn
Turner	Ronald Adam

Along with *Kind Hearts and Coronets* and *Passport to Pimlico*, this is one of the best things Ealing Studios ever produced. A meek clerk dreams up a way to rob his employers – The Bank of England. Even without the delicious humour, this would be an enjoyable heist movie. But thanks to the wonderful tongue-in-cheek script and stand-out performances from Guinness and Holloway, the film is an absolute joy from the beginning until the very final moments. What a shame, though, that it was decreed that crime couldn't be seen to pay.

- When writer 'Tibby' Clarke was stumped for a way for Guinness to rob the Bank of England, he approached the Bank itself to see if they could help. His appointments form read: 'Information required on means of stealing gold bullion'. Amazingly, the Bank set up a committee to work out how somebody could gain access to their vaults.

- The film was banned in former Czechoslovakia and Hungary. It was also prohibited to be shown in Northern Rhodesia, apparently on the orders of the British Government, which felt it might undermine respect for the law there.

> 'I like the bullion office. It holds all I ever wished for.'

Question: *How did the gang get their gold out of the country?*

Lawrence of Arabia

(1962)

Director: David Lean

Length: 216 min   **Rating:** PG

Source: Autobiography, *The Seven Pillars of Wisdom* by T.E. Lawrence

T.E. Lawrence	Peter O'Toole
Sherif Ali	Omar Sharif
Prince Feisal	Alec Guinness
Auda Abu Tayi	Anthony Quinn
Gen. Allenby	Jack Hawkins
Jackson Bentley	Arthur Kennedy
The Bey	Jose Ferrer
Col. Harry Brighton	Anthony Quayle
Dryden	Claude Rains
Gen. Murray	Donald Wolfit
Farraj	Michel Ray

This epic tale of British war hero Lawrence leading the Arabs against the Turks in World War I is one of the greatest spectacles the cinema has produced. Although the photography and the use of the wide screen is breathtaking, as is the score by Maurice Jarre, much of its success is down to just one man, O'Toole. He gets across the determination and near madness of the man. See it on a big screen.

- The famous shot of Sharif approaching through the desert was actually carried out by a stand-in, until the moment for him to dismount.
- O'Toole lost two stone during filming but there were compensations: 'How many young men get to live with Bedouins for a year?'
- The producer Spiegel convinced Lean to finish the movie by arranging for it to be shown at the Royal Command Film Performance.

'He was a poet, a scholar and a mighty warrior. He was also the most shameless exhibitionist since Barnum and Bailey.'

Question: *What innovation was adopted by the Bedouins working on the film?*

Local Hero
(1983)

Director: Bill Forsyth

Length: 111 min   **Rating:** PG

Source: Screenplay by Bill Forsyth

Happer	Burt Lancaster
Mac	Peter Riegert
Ben	Fulton Mackay
Urquhart	Denis Lawson
Oldsen	Peter Capaldi
Geddes	Rikki Fulton
Victor	Christopher Rozycki
Marina	Jenny Seagrove
Stella	Jennifer Black
Ricky	John Gordon Sinclair

Utterly delightful, magical comedy from the director of
Gregory's Girl. Riegert is the oil executive sent to
Scotland to buy an entire fishing village so his company
can build a refinery. But playing politics with guys in
suits hasn't quite prepared him for the canniness of the
villagers' negotiating tactics. Just as Riegert succumbs to
the charms of the landscape, so you'll succumb to the
charms of this warm-hearted film, peopled with
wonderfully eccentric characters.

FROM THE PRODUCER OF THE ACADEMY AWARD WINNING 'CHARIOTS OF FIRE,' A BRILLIANT NEW FILM BY DAVID PUTTNAM.

- Apparently this was the main influence behind the TV series *Northern Exposure*.

- Lancaster's performance is a brilliant parody of many that he has played straight before: the rapacious industrial tycoon.

- The score was provided by Mark Knopfler who went and stayed at the hotel in the little Scottish fishing village in order to pick up the ambience. The soundtrack proved a hit in its own right.

'I came here as a student minister, and didn't ever get away again.'

Question: *Where was the film shot?*

The Madness of King George
(1994)

His Majesty Was All Powerful And All Knowing. But He Wasn't Quite All There

---

Director: Nicholas Hytner

Length: 107 min   **Rating:** PG

Source: Play, *The Madness of George III* by Alan Bennett

George III . . . . .Nigel Hawthorne
Queen Charlotte . . . . .Helen Mirren
Dr Willis . . . . .Ian Holm
Prince of Wales .Rupert Everett
Greville . . . . .Rupert Graves
Thurlow . . . . .John Wood
Lady Pembroke . . . . .Amanda Donohoe

This account of 'Farmer' George's first bout of madness is spellbinding, right from the sumptuous opening where the King is being readied for the opening of the Parliament. It has everything: tragedy, high comedy, love, madness, political intrigue, bizarre medical practices, all rendered in Bennett's inimitable style. Hawthorne is brilliant, and Rupert Everett rises to the occasion and gives the best performance of his career as the bored Prince of Wales. One of the best historical movies ever.

- Surely we can hear but not see trumpets during the performance of 'The Water Music' that Hawthorne wrecks?

- The statue outside St. Paul's Cathedral at the end is that of Queen Anne, not Queen Victoria, as many thought. So not a boo-boo.

- Although the play was called *The Madness of George III*, the title was changed for the movie in case American audiences thought that this was a sequel to two movies that they had never heard of.

'Good evening, Mr. King.' – 'Good evening, Mrs. King.'

Question: *What disease did the King really have?*

The Maltese Falcon

(1941)

He's As Fast On The Draw As He Is In The Drawing Room

Director: John Huston

Length: 100 min   **Rating:** PG

Source: Novel by Dashiell Hammett

Sam Spade	Humphrey Bogart
Brigid O'Shaughnessy	Mary Astor
Iva Archer	Gladys George
Joel Cairo	Peter Lorre
Kasper Gutman	Sydney Greenstreet
Wilmer Cook	Elisha Cook Jr.
Det. Lt. Dundy	Barton MacLane
Effie Perine	Lee Patrick
Det. Tom Polhaus	Ward Bond
Miles Archer	Jerome Cowan

While investigating the death of his partner, cynical private eye Sam Spade is drawn into the search for a priceless statue of a black bird. Nobody was ever better as the hard-bitten detective than Bogie, though he's helped by an outstanding supporting cast. Most detective stories don't bear repeated viewing once you know who's done it. This is one of those rarities that improves with age and repeated visits.

- This was John Huston's first film as director and he planned it meticulously in advance with storyboards, filming largely in sequence. It was adapted by getting a secretary to copy the novel in script format, keeping the dialogue intact.

- At 62, this was the first film for Greenstreet who, after starting out as a tea planter, had spent his life on stage.

- This is one of those movies which you think *must* have won at least one Oscar. But it didn't get any.

> 'Don't be too sure I'm as crooked as I'm supposed to be.'

Question: *Why didn't George Raft take the part?*

The Manchurian Candidate
(1962)

Director: John Frankenheimer

Length: 126 min   **Rating:** PG

Source: Novel by Richard Condon

Bennett Marco	Frank Sinatra
Raymond Shaw	Laurence Harvey
Rosie	Janet Leigh
Raymond's mother	Angela Lansbury

A war hero returns from the Korean War having been programmed by his captors to be an assassin. This nerve-tingling conspiracy thriller, brilliantly written, manages to fit in many satirical sideswipes along the way. Claustrophic and gripping, it features the performance of a lifetime from Angela Lansbury as the ultimate Mother from Hell.

• Although playing Harvey's mother, Lansbury was only three years older than him, 37 to his 34.

> 'His brain has not only been washed, as they say. It has been dry cleaned.'

Question: *Whose favourite film was this?*

M*A*S*H
(1970)

Director: Robert Altman

Length: 116 min   **Rating:** 15

Source: Novel by Richard Hooker

Hawkeye Pierce . . . . .Donald Sutherland
Trapper John McIntyre . . . . .Elliott Gould
Duke Forrest . . . . .Tom Skerritt
Maj. Hotlips Houlihan . . . . .Sally Kellerman
Maj. Frank Burns .Robert Duvall
Lt. Hot Dish . . . . .Jo Ann Pflug

Two doctors at a Mobile Army Surgical Hospital in the
Korean War try to make life for themselves as comfy as
possible while irritating the hell out of anyone behaving
in a vaguely military manner. This freewheeling, anarchic
comedy is still incredibly fresh and funny, hitting most of
its targets exactly where it hurts.

- Encouraging input and improvisation, Altman made the
  cast and crew live under canvas on the Fox lot, where
  they behaved rather like the characters in the movie.
- This is probably the only movie to have the end credits
  read out over a PA system.

Question: *What happened at the preview for the foreign
press?*

Miracle on 34th Street

(1947)

Director: George Seaton

Length: 96 min   **Rating:** U

Source: Story by Valentine Davies

Doris Walker	Maureen O'Hara
Fred Gailey	John Payne
Kris Kringle	Edmund Gwenn
Susan Walker	Natalie Wood
Judge Harper	Gene Lockhart
Mr Sawyer	Porter Hall
Charles Halloran	William Frawley
Thomas Mars	Jerome Cowan
Mother	Thelma Ritter
Postal employee	Jack Albertson

The ultimate Christmas movie. Although O'Hara's too practical a career woman to believe in Santa, she employs Santa-lookalike Kris Kringle in her department store. But things get complicated when he claims to be the *real* Father Christmas. Although it is a little sluggish in places, it's a terribly sweet and charming confection with several scenes that are pure movie magic. Is there *anybody* who can watch the final courtroom scene without the tears flowing?

- Not surprisingly, Macy's department store cooperated wholeheartedly with the film, shot around the Christmas of 1946. The studio didn't think much of it and, instead of waiting until the next Noel, they released it in June.

- Despite its unseasonal release in summer, the film was a great success.

- The 1994 remake was far better than it was given credit for, though it still pales beside the original.

> 'Now wait a minute, Susie. Just because every child can't get its wish, that doesn't mean there isn't a Santa Claus.'

Question: *How did Gimbel's department store react to the film?*

Mr Smith Goes to Washington

(1939)

Director: Frank Capra

Length: 125 min   **Rating:** U

Source: Story, *The Gentleman from Montana* by Lewis R. Foster

Saunders	Jean Arthur
Jefferson Smith	James Stewart
Sen. Joseph Paine	Claude Rains
Jim Taylor	Edward Arnold
Gov. Hubert Hopper	Guy Kibbee
Diz Moore	Thomas Mitchell
Chick McGann	Eugene Pallette
Ma Smith	Beulah Bondi
Sen. Fuller	H.B. Warner
Pres. of Senate	Harry Carey

An idealistic boy scout leader becomes a Senator but finds that in Washington playing corrupt political games takes precedence over doing good. Luckily, this is Frank Capra's world, one in which the little people *can* make a difference. It's rather corny in places, but it still packs a hell of a punch at times and brings tears to the eyes on more than one occasion. Stewart is, well, Stewart but let's not forget the cynical and utterly delightful Arthur.

- The film created a storm, with America's politicians up in arms against it. Some congressmen tried to get it withdrawn from release.

- Joseph P. Kennedy, then ambassador to Britain, thought it shouldn't be shown in Europe because it would undermine the morale of America's allies and be seen as propaganda for the Axis powers.

- The famous American broadcaster of the 30s and 40s, H.V. Kaltenborn, appears as himself.

> 'I wouldn't give you two cents for all your fancy rules if, behind them, they didn't have a little bit of plain, ordinary, everyday kindness and a little looking out for the other fellow, too.'

Question: *How many Oscar nominations did the film receive?*

Modern Times
(1936)

Director: Charles Chaplin

Length: 87 min   **Rating:** U

Source: Screenplay by Charles Chaplin

Tramp	Charles Chaplin
A Gamin	Paulette Goddard
Cafe owner	Henry Bergman
Mechanic	Chester Conklin
Big Bill	Stanley 'Tiny' Sanford
Gamin's sister	Gloria De Haven

Only Chaplin would have the chutzpah to bring out what is essentially a silent film nine years after the talkies had changed the movies forever. Although some consider this satire on the mechanized age a classic, any but the greatest Chaplin fans will surely now find it grossly sentimental and unfunny for long stretches. Most of the best comedy sequences are retreads of Chaplin's earlier two-reelers and even the great scene on the production line is a lift.

- Chaplin's voice was heard on screen for the first time singing in the nonsense song. Chaplin wrote all the music.
- This was the last appearance of Chaplin's tramp.
- The extraordinarily close similarities to René Clair's film *A Nous La Liberté* didn't escape that movie's producers. They started a suit for plagiarism but dropped it when Clair himself said that he was flattered.

'Cry, dammit, cry! Camera! Goddammit, get down on your knees and look up at me!' [Chaplin to Goddard]

Question: *Where was this film banned?*

Mutiny on the Bounty
(1935)

Director: Frank Lloyd

Length: 135 min   **Rating:** A

Source: Novels, *Mutiny on the Bounty* & *Men Against the Sea* by Charles Nordhoof & James Norman Hall

Capt. William Bligh ....Charles Laughton
1st Officer Fletcher Christian ....Clark Gable
Robert Byam ....Franchot Tone
Smith ....Herbert Mundin
Ellison ....Eddie Quillan
Bacchus ....Dudley Digges
Burkitt ....Donald Crisp
Sir Joseph Banks ....Henry Stephenson
Chief's daughter ....Movita
Capt. Nelson ....Francis Lister

By and large this most famous version of the true(ish) tale of 18th-century sailors mutinying against their martinet captain moves along with a fair wind behind it. But there's no denying that it gets becalmed in some stretches. The acting is great, though, with Laughton splendidly over the top in one of the most imitated of all movie roles. Credit must also go to Gable who gives the role far more depth than we might expect. It was remade in 1962, and again as *The Bounty* in 1984.

- The production was beset with difficulties. Not only were there arguments among the cast, but the humidity on location ruined some footage and valuable equipment.

- Laughton researched his part thoroughly, even going so far as to have uniforms run up for him by the firm that had outfitted Bligh and which was still in existence, insisting that they be exact copies of the original.

- This was the only instance when three actors from the same film, Gable, Laughton and Tone, were nominated for Best Actor Oscars.

'I'll take my chances against the law. You'll take yours against the sea.'

Question: *Why didn't Gable want to play the part?*

A Night at the Opera
(1935)

Director: Sam Wood

Length: 96 min   **Rating:** U

Source: Screenplay by George S. Kaufman & Morrie Ryskind

Otis B. Driftwood	Groucho Marx
Fiorello	Chico Marx
Tomasso	Harpo Marx
Rosa Castaldi	Kitty Carlisle
Ricardo Baroni	Allan Jones
Herman Gottlieb	Sig Rumann
Mrs Claypool	Margaret Dumont
Rodolfo Lassparri	Walter Woolf King
Captain	Edward Keane
Steward	Gino Corrado

The Marx Brothers wreak their usual havoc on the world of opera. Despite the dreadful songs from Jones and the twee love interest, it contains some of their greatest moments and is a more coherent movie than their earlier films. The hilarious stateroom scene on the boat is here, as is the business with The Party of the First Part and the backstage destruction of Il Trovatore. Bliss.

- This was the Marx Brothers' first movie at MGM after being sacked by Paramount.
- MGM production chief Irving Thalberg made them go out on the road, testing the gags and routines they planned to use on real audiences until they were sure they were right.
- The out-of-favour Buster Keaton worked on both this film and *A Day at the Races*.

> 'That's…that's in every contract. That's…that's what they call a sanity clause.' – 'Ha, ha, ha. You can't fool me. There ain't no Sanity Clause!'

Question: *What was significant about this Marx Brothers movie?*

North by Northwest
(1959)

Director: Alfred Hitchcock

Length: 136 min   **Rating:** U

Source: Screenplay by Ernest Lehman

Roger Thornhill	Cary Grant
Eve Kendall	Eva Marie Saint
Phillip Vandamm	James Mason
The Professor	Leo G. Carroll
Leonard	Martin Landau
Clara Thornhill	Jessie Royce Landis
Lester Townsend	Philip Ober
Valerian	Adam Williams
Handsome woman	Josephine Hutchinson
Victor Larrabee	Edward Platt

The ultimate comedy-thriller. Ad-man Grant finds his
life in danger when he is mistaken for a spy. This
delicious blend of thrills, humour, mystery and great
chases is full of memorable scenes, including the crop-
dusting plane and the climax on Mount Rushmore.
Although there's one desperately bad fake wood, at least
Hitch doesn't inflict any of his lousy back-projection
work on us to destroy the mood. Pretty damn perfect.

- Mount Rushmore had to be re-created in the studio for close-up work.

- Hitchcock intentionally wouldn't let the cast know the whole plot. He wanted them to seem bewildered and uncertain about what was going to happen.

- The United Nations refused permission for Hitchcock to film in their building. The shot of Grant entering it was taken with a hidden camera.

'This matter is best disposed of from a great height. Over water.'

Question: *What was the original title?*

Once Upon a Time in the West

(1969)

There Were Three Men In Her Life. One To Take Her...One To Love Her...And One To Kill Her

---

Director: Sergio Leone

Length: 165 min   **Rating:** U

Source: Screenplay by Sergio Leone & Sergio Donati

Frank	Henry Fonda
Jill McBain	Claudia Cardinale
Cheyenne	Jason Robards
'Harmonica'	Charles Bronson
Morton	Gabriele Ferzetti
Sheriff	Keenan Wynn
Stony	Woody Strode
Knuckles	Jack Elam
Barman	Lionel Stander
Brett McBain	Frank Wolff

This is Leone's best spaghetti western. Combining echoes of many famous others with an unfathomable plot about water rights, the film benefits from location shooting in John Ford's sacred Monument Valley, flamboyant camerawork and tough performances, including Cardinale. Morricone's wildly overblown score helps immeasurably. One to be seen in widescreen.

- When originally released in America, it was in a much shorter version so that more screenings could be fitted into each day.

- The opening credits last for 10 minutes, making it the joint record-holder with *Superman* for the lengthiest, although that film splits them whereas Leone's has them all in one chunk during the opening 14-minute scene.

'How can you trust a man who wears both a belt and suspenders? Man can't even trust his own pants'

Question: *What year was the complete version released?*

One Flew Over the Cuckoo's Nest
(1975)

Director: Milos Forman

Length: 133 min   **Rating:** 18

Source: Novel by Ken Kesey & play by Dale Wasserman

Randle P. McMurphy	Jack Nicholson
Nurse Ratched	Louise Fletcher
Harding	William Redfield
Chief Bromden	Will Sampson
Billy Bibbit	Brad Dourif
Ellis	Michael Berryman
Taber	Christopher Lloyd
Martini	Danny DeVito
Col. Matterson	Peter Brocco
Turkle	Scatman Crothers

A prisoner thinks life will be cushier if he fakes madness. But although he tries to brighten up life at the mental institution he is transferred to, he meets implacable opposition from the sadistic head nurse. This deeply black comedy about rebellion and the power of the human spirit is a breath-taking experience, one of those rare films that seems to hit all the right buttons, making for electrifying entertainment.

- Kirk Douglas was very successful in the stage version of the play in the 60s. But his attempts to get the movie off the ground over more than a decade failed. By the mid 70s, he was too old to play the lead role. But son Michael managed to get it made.

- Dean R. Brooks, playing Dr John Spivey, was the superintendent of the Oregon State Hospital where the movie was made.

- Rumour has it that Nicholson disappeared for two months before filming started. When the crew arrived at the hospital to begin setting their equipment up, they found he had admitted himself as a voluntary patient.

'Medication time.'

Question: *How were some of the extras recruited?*

On the Waterfront

(1954)

Director: Elia Kazan

Length: 108 min   **Rating:** PG

Source: Pulitzer Prize-winning articles by Malcolm Johnson

Terry Malloy	Marlon Brando
Edie Doyle	Eva Marie Saint
Father Barry	Karl Malden
Johnny Friendly	Lee J. Cobb
Charley Malloy	Rod Steiger
'Kayo' Dugan	Pat Henning
Glover	Leif Erickson
Big Mac	James Westerfield

A still-impressive story of Union skullduggery in New York, with Marlon Brando standing up to the bully boys in between caring for his pigeons and wooing Eva Marie Saint. Once famed for its location realism, Elia Kazan's direction now looks rather arty. But the acting is still very impressive, and not only from The Great Mumbler himself. The underlying message about the need to be an informant remains controversial.

• Director Kazan admitted that the film was a penance for turning informer himself and testifying before the House Un-American Activities Committee.

- During the famous taxi scene, Rod Steiger stayed around on the set so that Brando would have someone to play off during his 'contender' speech. However, when it was time for Steiger to perform his part of the scene, he was faced not by Brando, who had already gone home, but by an assistant director.

- As originally written, Brando was to have been killed by the bent union officials. Crime could still not be seen to win, so the ending had to be altered.

> 'I could've had class. I could've been a contender. I could've been somebody, instead of a bum, which is what I am.'

Question: *How many oscars did this film win?*

The Producers
(1968)

Director: Mel Brooks

Length: 88 min   **Rating:** PG

Source: Screenplay by Mel Brooks

Max Bialystock	Zero Mostel
Leo Bloom	Gene Wilder
Frank Liebkind	Kenneth Mars
Lorenzo St Du Bois	Dick Shawn
Ulla	Lee Meredith
'Hold me, touch me'	Estelle Winwood
Roger De Bris	Christopher Hewett
Carmen Giya	Andreas Voutsinas
Drunk	William Hickey
Eva Braun	Renee Taylor

An ageing theatrical producer with a cardboard belt realizes that if a production flops he can keep all the money raised. With a pro-Hitler musical written by a Nazi and starring an amnesiac hippy, how can he go wrong? This hilarious monument to bad taste has now been recognized as one of great comedy classics. Get any two devotees together in a room and they'll invariably act out their favourite scenes. You should be warned that there could be many.

- Despite winning the Oscar for the Best Screenplay, the film was a flop on first release and only emerged from obscurity after the success of *Blazing Saddles*.
- The rows between Brooks and Mostel have gone down in Hollywood lore as being among the most furious in the industry's history.
- The voice in 'Springtime for Hitler' saying 'Don't be stupid, be a smarty, Come and join the Nazi Party' is that of Brooks.

'How could this happen? I was so careful. I picked the wrong play, the wrong director, the wrong cast. Where did I go right?'

Question: *What was the film's original title?*

Psycho
(1960)

Don't Give Away The Ending...It's The Only One We Have

Director: Alfred Hitchcock

Length: 109 min   **Rating:** 15

Source: Novel by Robert Bloch

Norman Bates .Anthony Perkins
Marion Crane . . . . .Janet Leigh
Lila Crane . . . . .Vera Miles
Sam Loomis . . . . .John Gavin
Milton Arbogast . . . . .Martin Balsam
Sheriff Chambers . . . . .John McIntire
Dr Richmond .Simon Oakland
Tom Cassidy . . . . .Frank Albertson
Caroline . . . . .Patricia Hitchcock
Mrs. Chambers . . . . .Lurene Tuttle

A woman on the run stops at the Bates Motel, where the main provision is a hot and cold running maniac with a mother fixation. Filmed cheaply and looking as if it was destined for the TV, this pulse-quickening, stomach-churning thriller is still an excellent remedy for narcolepsy. Oddly, it actually gets more frightening on future viewings, even though Hitch's jet-black humour is also then more apparent.

- Although Hitchcock had never made a horror movie before, this one established the slasher genre. One of his reasons for making the movie was his curiosity in seeing what happened if you killed off the star early in the film.

- One of the most famous sequences in movies, the shower scene, lasts only 45 seconds, involved 78 shots and took seven days to get in the can.

- To test how frightening 'mother' was, Hitch put her in Leigh's dressing room and waited to see how loudly she screamed.

'Mother...what's the phrase?...isn't quite herself today.'

Question: *Where is Hitchcock's cameo appearance?*

Pulp Fiction
(1994)

Director: Quentin Tarantino

Length: 153 min   **Rating:** 18

Source: Screenplay by Quentin Tarantino

Vincent Vega	John Travolta
Jules	Samuel L. Jackson
Mia	Uma Thurman
The Wolf	Harvey Keitel
Pumpkin	Tim Roth
Honey Bunny	Amanda Plummer
Fabienne	Maria De Madeiros
Marsellus Wallace	Ving Rhames
Lance	Eric Stoltz
Jody	Rosanna Arquette
Butch	Bruce Willis

Although it's overlong and plays a few too many tricks with cinema conventions, this more than amply demonstrates that *Reservoir Dogs* was no flash in the pan. Packed with Tarantino's witty, fizzing dialogue, it cleverly weaves together three stories set deep within the gore found inside the underbelly of American society. Although Jackson and Travolta were lauded for their roles, let's not forget how wonderful Willis is as the boxer told to throw a fight. Hugely entertaining, but be warned that it is pretty violent in places.

- It was hoped that Travolta would be at the Japanese opening. But he wanted to fly his own jet over and, when nobody volunteered to pay the $100,000 fuel cost, he refused to go, even first class.

- Although Willis gets $15m for *Die Hard* movies, he worked for minimum wages on this, getting just $1,400. In Cannes, he threw the dinner to celebrate the movie winning the Palme D'Or and probably ended up $100,000 poorer after making the film.

- The film started a run on stocks of Chanel Rouge Noir nail varnish, as used by Uma Thurman in the movie.

> 'Come on. Let's get in character.'

Question: *Who are the boxers in the support bout?*

Raging Bull
(1980)

Director: Martin Scorsese

Length: 128 min   **Rating:** 18

Source: Book by Jake La Motta with Joseph Carter & Peter Savage

Jake La Motta	Robert De Niro
Vicki	Cathy Moriarty
Joey	Joe Pesci
Salvy	Frank Vincent
Tommy	Nicholas Colasanto
Lenore	Theresa Saldana

In this downbeat biog of selfish, self-destructive boxer Jake La Motta, De Niro gives an amazing portrayal of a man whose animal side lurks just below the surface, ever ready to erupt. No punches are pulled in the often repellent boxing scenes. Although technically brilliant and voted by many critics their favourite 80s movie, De Niro plays so unsympathetic a character that the experience is not just bleak and uncomfortable, but also rather nasty.

- Throwing himself into the role as always, De Niro trained with La Motta for six months, putting on 50 pounds to play the boxer in his later years. La Motta

claimed that if De Niro ever tired of acting, he would acquit himself well in the boxing ring as a middleweight.

- Moriarty, a model, had never acted before. She was discovered by Pesci, who thought she looked identical to La Motta's wife.

- Pesci himself was running a restaurant when Scorsese persuaded him to do the movie.

> 'C'mon. You're my brother. Be friends, ya fuckin' bum. Give me a break. C'mon, kiss me. Give me a kiss. C'mon.'

Question: *Why did the real La Motta bill the film company?*

Rear Window
(1954)

Director: Alfred Hitchcock

Length: 112 min   **Rating:** PG

Source: Story, *It Had to Be Murder* by Cornell Woolrich

L.B. 'Jeff' Jeffries	James Stewart
Lisa Fremont	Grace Kelly
Det. Thomas J. Doyle	Wendell Corey
Stella	Thelma Ritter
Lars Thorwald	Raymond Burr
Miss Lonelyhearts	Judith Evelyn

A photographer with his leg in plaster spends his time gazing out of the window and comes to suspect one of his neighbours of murder. This is a great suspense movie made all the more gripping by the claustrophobia of the single set. Even as we watch it, we feel uncomfortable that we are slipping so easily into the role of voyeur. Among the added bonuses to this great film are the wisecracking Thelma Ritter, Grace Kelly at her sexiest best and the great soundtrack. Listen out for appropriate songs like 'Lisa' and 'To See You Is To Love You'.

• This is one of the five 'lost Hitchcocks'. Along with *Rope*, *The Man Who Knew Too Much* (1956), *Vertigo*

and *The Trouble with Harry*, the rights were bought back by Hitch as a legacy for his daughter.

- They were unseen for around 30 years, only being re-released in the mid-80s.

- One of the early ads for the film read, 'If you do not experience delicious terror when you see *Rear Window*, then pinch yourself – you are most probably dead.'

> 'We've become a race of Peeping Toms. What people ought to do is get outside their own house and look in for a change.'

Question: *Where is Hitchcock's cameo this time?*

Rocky
(1976)

Director: John G. Avildsen

Length: 119 min   **Rating:** PG

Source: Screenplay bySylvester Stallone

Rocky Balboa . . . . .Sylvester Stallone
Adrian . . . . .Talia Shire
Mickey . . . . .Burgess Meredith
Paulie . . . . .Burt Young
Apollo Creed . . . . .Carl Weathers
Miles Jergens . . . . .Thayer David

Although the plot could belong to any one of a hundred boxing movies, this tale of the underdog boxer getting a shot at the big one sweeps you up and carries you along with it until you're punching the air as the big boys are punching each other. With a charming accompanying love story and a fair helping of sentiment, this is an incredibly uplifting film.

- The fight scenes were filmed by three cameras, one of which was a hand-held Steadicam.

> 'Apollo Creed meets The Italian Stallion. Sounds like a damn monster movie.'

Question: *What event inspired the story ?*

Scarface
(1932)

Director: Howard Hawks	
Length: 99 min	**Rating:** 15
Source: Novel by Armitage Traill	

Tony Camonte	Paul Muni
Cesca Camonte	Ann Dvorak
Guino Rinaldo	George Raft
Gaffney	Boris Karloff
Poppy	Karen Morey

The third of the original trilogy of Gat Pack movies, along with *Little Caesar* and *Public Enemy*. This is a thinly-veiled portrait of Al Capone, with the gangster portrayed as an out-and-out murderer who hasn't even got society to blame for his behaviour. His only Achilles' heel is his near incestuous relationship with his sister.

• It appeared after *Little Caesar* and *Public Enemy*, because it was held back for over a year due to difficulties with the censors.

• After word of it got out that the film was really about Al Capone, writer Hecht was visited by two of Capone's henchmen. With his knowledge of Chicago gangster life from his days as a reporter, he managed to persuade them that it was about another gangster altogether.

Question: *What did Capone think of the film?*

Schindler's List

(1993)

Whoever Saves One Life Saves The World Entire

Director: Steven Spielberg
Length: 195 min
Source: Novel by Thomas Keneally

Oskar Schindler	Liam Neeson
Itzhak Stern	Ben Kingsley
Amon Goeth	Ralph Fiennes
Emilie Schindler	Caroline Goodall
Poldek Pfefferberg	Jonathan Sagalle
Helen Hirsch	Embeth Davidtz

Based on a true story, a Nazi industrialist protects his workers from The Final Solution. The use of hand-held cameras gives the film a documentary flavour and the story is grippingly and convincingly told. Fiennes is a particular standout as one of the most complex, vicious and almost pitiable villains in movie history. The film is moving, heart-rending and life-affirming. Although the Holocaust is not trivialized, the movie is less depressing than might be expected both because this is one tale that has a happy ending and because it is shot through with wry humour. What's more, it improves on further viewings. This is simply one of the most remarkable movies ever made.

- Spielberg had to fight long and hard to persuade Universal to allow him to make it in black and white, the industry view being that colour films will always make more money.

- Spielberg was refused permission to film inside Auschwitz. The set was built *beside* the real location and the train seen is actually moving *out* of Auschwitz rather than into it.

'What if I got here five minutes later? Then where would I be?'

Question: *What other film was Spielberg working on?*

The Searchers
(1956)

Director: John Ford

Length: 119 min   **Rating:** PG

Source: Novel by Alan LeMay

Ethan Edwards	John Wayne
Martin Pawley	Jeffrey Hunter
Laurie Jorgensen	Vera Miles
Capt. Rev. Sam Clayton	Ward Bond
Debbie Edwards	Natalie Wood
Lars Jorgensen	John Qualen
Brad Jorgensen	Harry Carey Jr.
Emilio Figueroa	Antonio Moreno
Mrs Jorgensen	Olive Carey
Chief Scar	Henry Brandon

The Western that film buffs go into raptures over.
Wayne is the bigoted ex-Confederate who searches for
seven years for the daughter of his brother and sister-in-
law who was taken prisoner by the Indians who
murdered her parents. While it's true that it's extremely
beautiful and that Wayne gives an untypically deep
performance, if you aren't reading deep, deep meaning
into it all the time, it can also be somewhat tedious in
places. I keep rewatching it, though.

- John Wayne was so taken with his character in this film, which he considered his best, that he named his third son John Ethan.

- The part of Debbie as a child was played by Natalie Wood's younger sister, Lana. She was later admirably to flesh out the role of Plenty O'Toole in *Diamonds Are Forever*.

- Something of a cult classic, this film is alluded to or quoted in many others, including *Taxi Driver* and *Star Wars*.

> 'That'll be the day.'

Question: *What are the names of the two Indian tribes that figure in this film?*

Singin' in the Rain
(1952)

Director: Gene Kelly & Stanley Donan

Length: 103 min   **Rating:** U

Source: Screenplay by Adolph Green & Betty Comden; Songs by Arthur Freed

Don Lockwood	Gene Kelly
Cosmo Brown	Donald O'Connor
Kathy Selden	Debbie Reynolds
Lina Lamont	Jean Hagen
R.F. Simpson	Millard Mitchell
Dancer	Cyd Charisse
Zelda Zanders	Rita Moreno
Roscoe Dexter	Douglas Fowley
Dora Bailey	Madge Blake
Rod	King Donovan

A boisterous, fizzing firecracker of a musical. This tale of the early days of talking pictures is pure cinematic magic. The story, of a young actress forced to dub the voice of an obnoxious silent star, is often extremely funny. The acting is splendid, with Kelly and O'Connor making a great buddy team while Gene and Debbie strike great sparks off each other. Some of the musical numbers are simply out of this world. The sort of movie you want to watch all over again as soon as you've seen it.

- The film received two Oscar nominations but didn't win one. *An American in Paris*, also starring Kelly, won the Best Picture Oscar that year.

- Before this film, Reynolds' dancing and singing experience was almost zero while Kelly and O'Connor had been performing since they could walk. In addition to his own taps, Kelly also dubbed those for Reynolds.

- The staging of the 'Singin' in the Rain' number was Kelly's idea. He asked for holes to be dug in the ground so that the water would collect in puddles.

> 'If we bring a little joy into your humdrum lives, it makes us feel our work ain't been in vain fer nothin.'

Question: *What did they add to the rain to make it show up better on film?*

Snow White and the Seven Dwarfs

(1937)

The Show Sensation of the Generation!

Director: Various

Length: 83 min   **Rating:** U

Source: Fairy tale by the Brothers Grimm

Snow White . . . . .Adriana Caselotti
Prince Charming . . . . .Harry Stockwell
The Queen . . . . .Lucille La Verne
Sneezy . . . . .Billy Gilbert

A beautiful princess fleeing her evil step-mother bunks down with seven besotted but extraordinarily well-behaved little diamond miners and ends up being rescued by the usual wimpish prince on a white horse. The lashings of sentiment in the first ever feature-length cartoon are now a little hard to take in places. However, there's ample compensation in the charming animation, the dwarfs' humour, the timeless songs and the truly scary Queen.

• So certain was Hollywood that the public wouldn't sit still for a feature cartoon that the project was dubbed 'Disney's folly'.

- In Britain, there was a censorship storm, with the flight of Snow White through the forest considered so frightening that nobody under the age of 16 could see it unless accompanied by an adult.

- This was the first screen musical to generate its own soundtrack album.

- When Disney received a special award for the movie, Shirley Temple handed over a regular Oscar, together with seven little ones.

'Mirror, mirror, on the wall, who is the fairest of them all?'

Question: *What are the names of the Seven Dwarfs?*

Some Like It Hot
(1959)

Director: Billy Wilder

Length: 120 min   **Rating:** PG

Source: Screenplay, *Fanfares of Love*, by Robert Thoeren & M. Logan

Sugar Kane	Marilyn Monroe
Joe/Josephine	Tony Curtis
Jerry/Daphne	Jack Lemmon
Osgood E. Fielding III	Joe E. Brown
Spats Columbo	George Raft
Mulligan	Pat O'Brien
Little Bonaparte	Nehemiah Persoff
Sweet Sue	Joan Shawlee
Toothpick Charlie	George E. Stone
Spat's henchman	Mike Mazurki

Two musicians witness the Valentine's Day Massacre and hide out in drag with an all girl jazz band. As one of them is the insufferably gorgeous Marilyn Monroe, life in womens' clothing proves something of a strain. A splendid re-creation of the Jazz Age, this is as nearly perfect as a comedy can be. The script is lively, witty and imaginative, the action moves at a smart lick and the performances from Lemmon, Curtis and particularly Monroe, are out of this world.

- The film was planned to star Danny Kaye and Bob Hope. Then Lemmon was signed, only to be sacked when it looked as if Frank Sinatra would sign up. When Monroe agreed to star, however, Sinatra was not needed and Lemmon was back in. Monroe's signing meant Mitzi Gaynor was booted out.

- Monroe apparently agreed to do the film without reading the script. Once she did, she was horrified that she was being asked to play a blonde so dumb she couldn't tell her two girlfriends were men in drag.

- Ex-Broadway dancer Raft taught Lemmon and Joe E. Brown how to tango for their scene together.

> 'I think you're on the right track.' – 'I must be. Your glasses are beginning to steam up.'

Question: *On whom is 'Josephine' based?*

Stagecoach
(1939)

Director: John Ford

Length: 96 min   **Rating:** U

Source: Short story, *Stage to Lordsburg* by Ernest Haycox

Dallas	Claire Trevor
The Ringo Kid	John Wayne
Dr Josiah Boone	Thomas Mitchell
Hatfield	John Carradine
Buck Rickabaugh	Andy Devine
Sheriff Curly Wilcox	George Bancroft
Mr. Samuel Peacock	Donald Meek
Lucy Mallory	Louise Platt
Lt. Blanchard	Tim Holt
Henry Gatewood	Berton Churchill

The Western everybody seems to like. In essence, it's just a group of seven people with assorted problems who are crammed into a tiny room. However, the 'room' is on its way through Indian territory while the savages are on the warpath. Sure enough, the Indians attack and the scene is set for some exciting action. It could so easily have been another B-Western, but the mix gelled and what came out the other end was a classic that has endured and will continue to enchant moviegoers.

- Ford had earlier given Wayne, a few bit parts. Since then he had been appearing only in B-Westerns. There was considerable opposition to Wayne being offered the part.

- Ford insisted on paying the Navajo extras the same as everyone else, against the opposition of the front office. Ford was afterwards made an honorary Navajo chief.

- The original prints of *Stagecoach* all disappeared over the years and the current prints of the film were struck from John Wayne's own copy in 1970.

> 'Somewhere, sometime, there may be the right bullet or the wrong bottle waiting for Josiah Boone. Why worry when or where?'

Question: *Why was it hard to edit Ford's films?*

Star Wars

(1977)

Director: George Lucas

Length: 121 min   **Rating:** U

Source: Screenplay by George Lucas

Luke Skywalker	Mark Hamill
Han Solo	Harrison Ford
Princess Leia Organa	Carrie Fisher
Ben Obi-Wan Kenobi	Alec Guinness
Grand Moff Tarkin	Peter Cushing
C3PO	Anthony Daniels
R2-D2	Kenny Baker
Lord Darth Vader	David Prowse
Darth Vader's voice	James Earl Jones
Chewbacca	Peter Mayhew

Rebels loyal to a beautiful princess take on the evil Empire, with the help of a knight trained by a wise old man. Although transferred into outer space, this is an old, old story and that's probably the reason for its amazing success. It's the believable fight between good and evil that ensures we can watch it again and again, not the expensive FX. Some of these effects now look a little dated and the jokey robots eventually become irritating. These are only minor drawbacks, though, to a cracking adventure yarn which works up to a terrifically exciting finale.

- The John Williams soundtrack became the highest-selling original soundtrack ever.

- The swing with Hamill across the chasm in the Death Star terrified Fisher. They were actually 30 feet up and weren't allowed to use doubles. Fortunately, they got it right on the first take.

- James Earl Jones asked not to be credited, feeling he hadn't done enough work to justify it. Rumour has it that David Prowse had not been told that his voice would be dubbed.

- It was never originally planned to be anything more than a one-off, except perhaps in Lucas' imagination.

'May the Force be with you!'

Question: *Why did Lucas quit the Directors' Guild?*

The Sting

(1973)

All It Takes Is A Little Confidence

Director: George Roy Hill

Length: 129 min   **Rating:** PG

Source: Screenplay by David S. Ward

Henry Gondorff	Paul Newman
Johnny Hooker	Robert Redford
Doyle Lonnegan	Robert Shaw
Lt. William Snyder	Charles Durning
J.J. Singleton	Ray Walston
Billie	Eileen Brennan
Kid Twist	Harold Gould
Eddie Niles	John Heffernan
FBI Agent Polk	Dana Elcar
'Erie Kid'	Jack Kehoe

A pair of confidence tricksters go for the big one, avenging a friend's death by setting up a Chicago gangster. Re-teaming the actors who had made *Butch Cassidy and the Sundance Kid* with the same director, this film hit it big at the box office. It has a wonderful 30s atmosphere, thanks in large part to Marvin Hamlisch's revival of Scott Joplin's music. There's also a humdinger of a plot, clever in its construction and immensely enjoyable in its execution.

- The film was the first in over 25 years to begin with the Universal logo of the glass globe which had been the studio's hallmark in the 40s.

- The hands in the poker game seen close-to are not Newman's but card guru John Scarne's.

- Although Scott Joplin's music now seems irretrievably linked with the movie, it isn't of the right period. Rather than the 30s, ragtime was all the rage around the turn of the century, a generation earlier.

> 'He's not as tough as he thinks.' – 'Neither are we.'

Question: *How many Oscars did the film win?*

Sunset Boulevard
(1950)

A Hollywood Story

Director: Billy Wilder

Length: 110 min   **Rating:** PG

Source: Screenplay by Billy Wilder, Charles Brackett & D.M. Marshman Jr.

Joe Gillis	William Holden
Norma Desmond	Gloria Swanson
Max von Mayerling	Erich von Stroheim
Betty Schaefer	Nancy Olson
Sheldrake	Fred Clark
Morino	Lloyd Gough
Artie Green	Jack Webb
Himself	Cecil B. DeMille
Herself	Hedda Hopper
Himself	Buster Keaton

A scriptwriter with no cash or prospects goes to work on a futile project for a former silent movie star with extreme delusions of fame and grandeur. But eventually he wakes up to the fact that he is virtually being held a prisoner by the woman and her menacing butler. Although it pleases as straight storytelling, this is a multi-layered film, with elements of melodrama, satire, gothic horror and black humour woven in. It is also one

of the most interesting and insightful peeps behind the curtain of Hollywood, rendered still more fascinating by the use of many of the true stars of the silent era.

- When the film opened at the Radio City Music Hall, the queue stretched for three blocks.

- The mansion in the movie belonged to the Getty family and wasn't at 10086 Sunset but 3810 Wilshire Boulevard. The film-makers built a swimming pool there in return for the use of the place.

- 52-year-old Swanson was unhappy at having to test for the part, but eventually agreed.

'We didn't need dialogue. We had *faces* then.'

Question: *What was odd about Von Stroheim playing a chauffeur?*

Taxi Driver
(1976)

On Every Street In Every City, There's A Nobody Who Dreams Of Being A Somebody

Director: Martin Scorsese

Length: 113 min   **Rating:** 18

Source: Screenplay by Paul Schrader

Travis Bickle	Robert De Niro
Betsy	Cybill Shepherd
Iris Steensman	Jodie Foster
Wizard	Peter Boyle
Sport	Harvey Keitel
Tom	Albert Brooks
Charles Palantine	Leonard Harris
Man in taxi	Martin Scorsese
Personnel officer	Joe Spinell
Concession girl	Diahnne Abbott

An inarticulate Vietnam veteran, now a taxi driver, is dehumanized and brutalized by the crime and sordid behaviour he sees around him. When he comes across a young prostitute, he vows to rescue her from her predicament. De Niro's edgy, surprisingly sympathetic, performance is electrifying and the depiction of the underbelly of New York life sordid and realistic. This is a bleak and uncompromising film.

- The producers couldn't find a major studio to back the movie unless Jeff Bridges played the part of Bickle. But when writer Schrader saw *Mean Streets*, he knew he'd found the right director. His addition to the team persuaded Columbia to back the movie.

- The 'You talkin' to me?' scene was ad-libbed by De Niro.

- Jodie Foster not only had to be checked out by a psychiatrist before filming but was accompanied everywhere by a social worker during production.

> 'All the animals come out at night: whores, scum, pussies, buggers, queens, fairies, dopers, junkies. Sick. Venal. Some day a real rain will come and wash this scum off the streets.'

Question: *How did De Niro prepare for his role?*

The Terminator

(1984)

Director: James Cameron

Length: 108 min   **Rating:** 18

Source: Screenplay by Gale Anne Hurd & James Cameron

Terminator	Arnold Schwarzenegger
Kyle Reese	Michael Biehn
Sarah Connor	Linda Hamilton
Traxler	Paul Winfield
Vukovich	Lance Henriksen
Matt	Rick Rossovich
Ginger	Bess Motta
Silberman	Earl Boen
Pawn shop clerk	Dick Miller
Punk leader	Bill Paxton

Highly influential sci-fi thriller with Arnie in pre-superstar days as an evil cyborg, sent back from the future to stop a potential rebel leader being born to a bewildered Linda Hamilton. One of those rare films in which splendid action sequences are complemented by an intelligent and witty script. It holds up brilliantly no matter how many times you watch it, even if some of the stop-motion special effects now look a mite ropey.

- Harlan Ellison successfully sued, claiming the plot came from an *Outer Limits* TV episode he wrote.

- O.J. Simpson was considered for the terminator's role, but the film-makers worried that audiences wouldn't take him seriously.

- Henriksen and Schwarzenegger originally had each other's roles. After reading the script, Arnie asked to swop over.

'I'll be back.'

Question: *How many Sarah Connors were there?*

The Third Man
(1949)

Director: Carol Reed
Length: 104 min   **Rating:** PG
Source: Screenplay by Graham Greene

Holly Martins	Joseph Cotten
Harry Lime	Orson Welles
Anna Schmidt	Alida Valli
Maj. Calloway	Trevor Howard
Sgt. Paine	Bernard Lee
Crabbin	Wilfrid Hyde-White
'Baron' Kurtz	Ernst Deutsch
British policeman	Geoffrey Keen
Porter	Paul Hoerbiger

A perfect movie? As near as they come. Writer Cotten searches for an old friend in devastated postwar Vienna, not realizing what sort of man he'd turned into. A cracking yarn made flesh by outstanding acting, a fantastic sense of time and place, pacey direction and superlative photography. Maybe a touch less of the evocative zither music wouldn't have hurt. One of those rare films that can be watched again and again.

- Trevor Howard claimed to have discovered Anton Karas playing zither outside a restaurant in Vienna.

- Many think that Welles came up with much of his own dialogue but, with the exception of writing the speech about cuckoo clocks, in fact he largely stuck to the script as written.

- Filming for just five weeks in occupied Vienna was difficult, so the crew was divided into two, a day crew and a night crew. Reed had to be around all the time, and survived the shoot with just a couple of brief naps each day.

> 'What can I do, old man? I'm dead, aren't I?'

Question: *Who had been first choice to play Harry Lime?*

The 39 Steps
(1935)

Director: Alfred Hitchcock

Length: 85 min   **Rating:** U

Source: Novel by John Buchan

Richard Hannay ....Robert Donat
Pamela ....Madeleine Carroll
Miss Smith ....Lucie Mannheim
Prof. Jordan ....Godfrey Tearle
Crofter's wife ....Peggy Ashcroft

A Canadian on holiday in London is pitched into a search for enemy spies, even while he is being hunted by the authorities as a murderer. Although some of the sets now look a bit ropey, it remains a great chase movie with lashings of comic touches, wonderful thrills, deft dialogue and the still sexy predicament of Donat and the reluctant Carroll handcuffed together. Remade in 1959 and 1978, neither can hold a candle to it.

- Hitch can be glimpsed five or six minutes from the opening, dropping litter as Donat and Mannheim flee from the music hall.

> 'There are twenty million women in this island and I've got to be chained to you.'

Question: *What was Hitchcock's practical joke on set?*

Top Hat
(1935)

Director: Mark Sandrich

Length: 101 min   **Rating:** U

Source: Musical, *The Gay Divorcee* by Dwight Taylor & Cole Porter, adapted from the play, *The Girl Who Dared* by Alexander Farago & Aladar Laszlo

Jerry Travers	Fred Astaire
Dale Tremont	Ginger Rogers
Horace Hardwick	Edward Everett Horton
Madge Hardwick	Helen Broderick
Alberto Beddini	Erik Rhodes
Bates, the butler	Eric Blore
Flower shop clerk	Lucille Ball

When dancer Astaire falls for Rogers, she believes he's actually her friend's husband and isn't too keen on his wooing her. Although the plot is second-hand, and the last quarter of an hour of the film comes across as rather rushed, Astaire and Rogers have an almost magical relationship here and the film contains some very funny scenes. Best of all is the Irving Berlin music.

• Rhodes' stereotypical Italian so offended Mussolini that this film was banned in Italy.

Question: *Who can be spotted as the clerk in the flower shop?*

2001: A Space Odyssey
(1968)
The Ultimate Trip

Director: Stanley Kubrick

Length: 141 min   **Rating:** U

Source: Short story, *The Sentinel* by Arthur C. Clarke

David Bowman ....Keir Dullea
Frank Poole ....Gary Lockwood
Dr Heywood Floyd ....William Sylvester
Moonwatcher ....Daniel Richter
Smyslov ....Leonard Rossiter
Voice of Hal 9000 ....Douglas Rain
Elena ....Margaret Tyzack
Mission controller ....Frank Miller
Halvorsen ....Robert Beatty

A spaceship is sent off to Jupiter in search of the
recipient of a signal sent from a black monolith on the
moon, but the computer and crew don't see eye to eye.
This visually arresting spectacle was generally held to be
deeply profound. It is still capable of filling us with
wonder at the majesty of the universe and man's
insignificance within it. Considering that it was made
before anyone had even walked on the moon, it is
remarkable how realistic the space sequences still look.

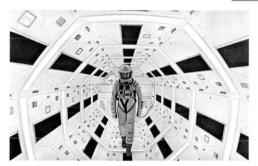

- Transpose HAL by one letter and you get IBM. Clarke and Kubrick claimed this was a coincidence. Kubrick said his original idea was to have a woman voice the computer, which was to be called Athena. When he changed his mind, the name came about from a combination of buzz-words 'heuristic' and 'algorithmic'.

- The Dawn of Man sequence used only two real baby chimpanzees. The rest were people in suits.

- Perhaps what has dated most is the idea that a person can fit comfortably inside a computer's memory bank.

> 'I'm sorry, Dave. I'm afraid I can't do that.'

Question: *How long into the film is it before there is any dialogue?*

Vertigo
(1958)

A Tall Story About A Pushover

Director: Alfred Hitchcock

Length: 128 min   **Rating:** PG

Source: Novel, *D'Entre les Morts* by Pierre Boileau & Thomas Narcejac

John 'Scottie' Ferguson	James Stewart
Madeleine/Judy	Kim Novak
Midge	Barbara Bel Geddes
Gavin Elster	Tom Helmore
Coroner	Henry Jones
Doctor	Raymond Bailey
Manageress	Ellen Corby
Pop Leibel	Konstantin Shayne
Older Mistaken Identity	Lee Patrick

Hitchcock baffled contemporary audiences with this slow, operatic love story of agoraphobic James Stewart falling for his client's blonde wife. The film's re-release in 1983 revealed a haunting, despairing portrait of romantic obsession which improves on each viewing. Stewart was seldom better and for once Kim Novak's artificiality is just right. It is now seen as one of Hitchcock's finest, most imitated films.

- When French writers Pierre Boileau and Thomas Narcejac heard that Alfred Hitchcock was interested in acquiring the rights to their book on which *Les Diaboliques* was based, they decided to write another novel specifically to interest him. The book, *From Among the Dead* in English, became *Vertigo*. Hitchcock only found out several years later that far from him cleverly spotting a good property, it had his name on it from the start.

- Hitchcock invented the famous combination of zooming the lens in while moving the camera backwards to create the sensation of vertigo to the audience. The view down the mission stairwell cost $19,000 to achieve for just a couple of seconds of screen time.

Question: *Where is Hitchcock's cameo appearance this time?*

Way Out West
(1937)

Director: James W. Horne

Length: 65 min   **Rating:** U

Source: Screenplay by Charles Rogers, James Parrott & Felix Adler

Stanley	Stan Laurel
Ollie	Oliver Hardy
Lola Marcel	Sharon Lynne
Mickey Finn	James Finlayson
Mary Roberts	Rosina Lawrence
Sheriff	Stanley Fields

In their finest feature film, Laurel and Hardy are sent West to deliver the deeds to a gold mine. Not unnaturally, there are a few hiccoughs in their mission. The film, in which their relationship seems terribly natural and touching, contains some of their best routines as well as the great song 'The Trail of the Lonesome Pine'. Best of all, though, is their hilarious little dance, 'Commencin' Dancing' on the steps of the saloon. Tear-weeping, side-splitting joy.

- Laurel and Hardy were having personal problems at the time and both separated from their wives during filming.

- The boys' rendition of 'The Trail of the Lonesome Pine' got to number two in the British charts in 1975.

- This was Laurel and Hardy's only Western spoof.

- The film was nominated for an Academy Award for Best Score.

'Now that you've got the mine, I'll bet you'll be a swell gold-digger.'

Question: *Who is their faithful companion?*

The Wild Bunch
(1969)

Director: Sam Peckinpah

Length: 144 min   **Rating:** 18

Source: Screenplay by Walon Green & Sam Peckinpah

Pike Bishop	William Holden
Dutch Engstrom	Ernest Borgnine
Deke Thornton	Robert Ryan
Sykes	Edmond O'Brien
Lyle Gorch	Warren Oates
Hector Gorch	Ben Johnson
Angel	Jaime Sanchez
Coffer	Strother Martin
T.C.	L.Q. Jones
Menacing man	Albert Dekker

After a failed armed robbery, a group of old-fashioned outlaws arrange one more do-or-die job so that they can retire. This film, set against the background of the Mexican Revolution, aroused enormous controversy over the extent of the violence. Those scenes will give few viewers pause for thought now and the film remains an elegiac sunset Western with some great action scenes. The atmosphere and detail is so rich that it is hard at times to remember that you are watching a movie rather than real life.

- After the film was shown to reviewers in the United States it was cut heavily by the studio while Sam Peckinpah was away on holiday. Although the previews had been positive, it appears the studio wanted a shorter film so that it could make more at the box office.

- 12,000 Red Harvester ants and 12 grey scorpions were imported to the Mexican location from Hollywood.

- Alfonso Arau, one of Mapache's lieutenants, later became a director of films such as *Like Water for Chocolate* and *A Walk in the Clouds*.

> 'It ain't like it used to be, but it'll do.'

Question: *How long did the censors take to pass the director's cut?*

The Wizard of Oz
(1939)

Director: Victor Fleming

Length: 101 min   **Rating:** U

Source: Book by Frank L. Baum

Dorothy	Judy Garland
Prof. Marvel/Wizard	Frank Morgan
Hunk/Scarecrow	Ray Bolger
Zeke/Cowardly Lion	Bert Lahr
Hickory/The Tin Man	Jack Haley
Glinda	Billie Burke
Miss Gulch/Wicked Witch	Margaret Hamilton
Uncle Henry	Charley Grapewin
Auntie Em	Clara Blandick

An unhappy girl runs away to the fantasy world of Oz and searches for happiness at the end of the Yellow Brick Road. The fondness so many feel for this musical may have a lot to do with nostalgia for a simpler age, but it is beautifully directed, with some neat performances and the good songs, like 'Somewhere Over the Rainbow' and 'We're Off to See the Wizard' really are humdingers.

- *Over the Rainbow* was added to the film very late on and, after previews, was ordered by the men in suits to be taken out again. Associate producer Arthur Freed said: 'The song stays – or I go! It's as simple as that.'

- The film-makers had planned painting the horse that takes our heroes to the Emerald City. But animal groups found out and protested. So the horses used had to be covered with coloured gelatine. Unfortunately, the animals loved the stuff and kept licking it off.

- One of the four identical pairs of ruby slippers was sold in 1988 for $165,000.

'Toto, I've a feeling we're not in Kansas anymore.'

Question: *How was the tornado created?*

QUIZ ANSWERS

The Adventures of Robin Hood: A giant park 350 miles northeast of LA. Fake trees and rocks were brought in to fill it.

African Queen: *Trader Horn* and *King Solomon's Mines*.

All About Eve: Davis only got the part when Claudette Colbert put her back out and had to be put in traction.

All Quiet on the Western Front: Trenches were dug on 20 acres of a ranch in California to simulate the battlefields, with 2000 extras recruited from ex-servicemen. Two miles of pipes were laid to carry the water necessary to make the land water-logged.

American Graffiti: 'THX 138' is virtually the title of Lucas' first feature film, *THX-1138*.

Annie Hall: He was playing clarinet in Michael's Pub in New York and he wasn't going to break his regular habit just to pick up an Oscar or two.

The Apartment: Adlibbing.

Apocalypse Now: *Apocalypse When?* because it took five years to make.

Arsenic and Old Lace: The filmmakers couldn't release it until the smash Broadway run of the play was over. It stayed on the shelf for almost three years as a result.

Ben Hur: Because Heston was the only one permitted by the director to have blue eyes.

The Best Years of Our Lives: He became the first of only two non-professionals to win an acting Oscar. In fact, Russell won two Oscars – the only person to do so for the same performance – because the Academy gave him a special award, only to find him winning Best Supporting Actor as well.

The Big Sleep: Hawks and Bogart argued over how the chauffeur had died. When asked, the writer is said to have replied: 'How should I know?'

Blade Runner: There's no right answer. You'll go mad trying to work it out.

Bonnie and Clyde: Bonnie's younger sister sued Warners for more than $1m for the blackening of her sibling's memory.

Breakfast at Tiffany's: *Follow That Blonde*.

Brief Encounter: Carnforth station in Lancashire.

Cabaret: Her hairstyle was modelled on that of Louise Brooks.

Casablanca: The drums.

Chinatown: The film was nominated for 11 Oscars, but only won the one for Best Screenplay.

Citizen Kane: Reportedly Welles saw *Stagecoach* 40 times to study moviemaking.

Dances With Wolves: A choke chain.

David Copperfield: By pinching her feet painfully out of the camera's view.

Dr Strangelove: Or How I Learned to Stop Worrying and Love the Bomb: *Fail-Safe*.

Double Indemnity: Amazingly, the film did not win a single Oscar.

Duck Soup: Margaret Dumont was actually bald. Harpo never tired throughout their career of stealing her wig.

Easy Rider: While the New Orleans scenes look as if they're intended to show how somebody who is high might see things, in fact it was an accident which left the film fogged.

E.T. The Extra-Terrestrial: By taking a picture of a baby and putting Albert Einstein's eyes and forehead on top.

Fantasia: Walt Disney himself.

42nd Street: Powell and Keeler went on to make another six musicals together, seven in all.

Frankenstein: Because there were no lines for the part, only grunts.

The French Connection: Egan appears in the film as Doyle's boss, Simonson. Hackman spent several weeks with Egan to study police work. Some real-life episodes involving the unconventional Egan appear in the movie.

From Here to Eternity: Joan Crawford, but she got involved in an argument about her costumes and scarpered.

Gaslight: Heddy Lamaar turned down the lead.

The General: The engine was recovered and shipped out for scrap during World War Two.

The Godfather: Sofia Coppola, director Francis Ford Coppola's daughter, who was later to star in the third part of the trilogy.

Goldfinger: Fort Knox really is Fort Knox, the filmmakers were granted permission to shoot on location, at least on the outside.

Gone with the Wind: Though barred from the premiere because it was held in a whites-only cinema, Butterfly McQueen (Prissy) was the guest of honour at the 50th anniversary celebrations.

Goodfellas: The previous record was held by the film *Scarface*.

The Graduate: Robert Redford, but he rejected it on the grounds that he thought no-one would believe he found it difficult to get to meet girls.

The Grapes of Wrath: Although initially welcomed in Russia because of its depiction of the downside of capitalism, it was then banned after Russians marvelled that the poorest of Americans could still afford a car.

A Hard Day's Night: The title came from John's description of Ringo's weird way with English. One all-night recording session was, according to him, 'a hard day's night'.

Henry V: A teenage George Cole.

High Noon: Writer Carl Foreman was blacklisted as a Communist after he was brought before the House Un-American Activities Committee during filming. He refused to name names or discuss his political affiliations and was forced to continue his career in Britain, where he wrote *Bridge on the River Kwai* and *The Guns of Navarone*.

In the Heat of the Night: Illinois and Tennessee, the latter standing in for Mississippi.

Intolerance: So many flames were shooting up when they filmed the night battle sequence that the local fire brigade turned out.

Invasion of the Body Snatchers: *Sleep No More*.

The Invisible Man: He didn't want to play a part where he couldn't largely be seen.

It's a Wonderful Life: None, though nominated for five Oscars.

Jaws: Three hydraulically-controlled sharks were made at a cost of $150,000 each.

Kind Hearts and Coronets: It was originally intended that Alec Guinness would play just four members of the D'Ascoyne family. Playing eight posed him some problems. 'I had to ask myself from time to time: "Which one am I now?" It would have been quite disastrous to have faced the camera in the make-up of the suffragette and spoken like the admiral.'

King Kong: Hitler said this was his favourite movie.

The Last Picture Show: *Father of the Bride* and *Red River*.

The Lavender Hill Mob: They melted it down and molded it into small souvenir Eiffel Towers to ship off to Paris.

Lawrence of Arabia: O'Toole learnt to ride a camel for the film, only becoming comfortable when he put a layer of foam rubber under the saddle blanket. It was an innovation that was then copied by Bedouin tribesman working on the movie.

Local Hero: The village of Pennan in northeast Scotland.

The Madness of King George: Porphyria – he wasn't mad at all.

The Maltese Falcon: He didn't think the picture 'important' enough and wasn't prepared to chance it with a novice director.

The Manchurian Candidate: Reportedly it was one of President John F. Kennedy's favourite movies.

M*A*S*H: There was a mass walkout at the sight of all the blood.

Miracle on 34th Street: Macy's big rival, Gimbel's, ran a full-page ad in the *New York Times* not only praising the film, but patting Macy's on the back for being involved.

Mr. Smith Goes to Washington: It received 11 Oscar nominations, but only won for Best Original Story.

Modern Times: Nazi Germany and Mussolini's Italy.

Mutiny on the Bounty: He didn't want to shave off his moustache and didn't like the idea of wearing wigs and silly trousers.

A Night at the Opera: It was their first film without Zeppo.

North by Northwest: According to Hitchcock: 'Our original title was "The Man in Lincoln's Nose".'

Once Upon a Time in the West: In 1984.

One Flew Over the Cuckoo's Nest: Through an ad in the local paper that said: 'Do you have a face that scares timber wolves?'

On the Waterfront: Eight Oscars.

The Producers: The original title was *Springtime for Hitler*.

Psycho: Hitchcock can be seen standing outside Leigh's office in a cowboy hat.

Pulp Fiction: The support fight for Willis' bout is 'Vossler vs. Martinez', these being the names of two of Tarantino's buddies from the video store days.

Raging Bull: De Niro had broken the caps on La Motta's teeth and he billed the film company the $4,000 for his dental bills.

Rear Window: Hitchcock appears roughly an hour into the movie, winding the clock in the songwriter's flat.

Rocky: The fight between part-time New Jersey boxer Chuck Wepner and Muhammad Ali. Although not expected to last long after the opening bell, the fight went 15 rounds.

Scarface: Capone enjoyed it so much he bought a print of it.

Schindler's List: After filming Schindler during the day in Poland, by night he was editing *Jurassic Park* using a satellite link.

The Searchers: The character Marin Pawley is part-Cherokee, and the Edwards girls were abducted a Comanche band.

Singin' in the Rain: They added milk to the rain.

Snow White and the Seven Dwarfs: Sneezy, Sleepy, Grumpy, Happy, Bashful, Dopey and Doc.

Some like it Hot: Curtis claims to have based his Josephine on Grace Kelly.

Stagecoach: Ford almost never attended rushes. He 'cut in the camera', only filming scenes as he intended them to appear, instead of from countless angles as other directors did. There was thus little opportunity for an editor to change Ford's vision of the movie.

Star Wars: The Directors' Guild of America told Lucas he had to put some credits at the beginning of the movie. Lucas refused, paid the fine they levied, and then quit the Guild.

The Sting: It won seven Oscars.

Sunset Boulevard: Von Stroheim couldn't drive, so when he appeared as Swanson's chauffeur, the car was being towed.

Taxi Driver: De Niro lost two-and-a-half stone and worked as a taxi driver to prepare for his role.

The Terminator: There were three women by that name in the phone book, and the evil Terminator gets to two of them. The heroine survives because she had gone out for the evening.

The Third Man: Noel Coward. Welles took the part to raise money for his film of *Othello*.

The 39 Steps: He handcuffed Carroll and Donat together on set to get them used to their film predicament and then left them, taking the key.

Top Hat: Lucille Ball, still playing bit parts in her 18th film.

2001: A Space Odyssey: There is no dialogue at all for the first 22 minutes.

Vertigo: Hitchcock appears 10 minutes in walking past the shipyard.

Way Out West: Their faithful friend is a mule.

The Wild Bunch: It took almost two years. When the director's cut was shown to the censors in 1992, they threatened to give it an NC-17 certificate, the kiss of death in American cinemas, even though it had only been an R in 1969 and no scenes of violence had been added. The battle over its certificate lasted until late 1994 before it was allowed to keep the R rating.

The Wizard of Oz: By swirling, not a lady's stocking as some have said, but a 35-foot muslin wind sock in front of the camera.

Picture Credits

ABC/Allied Artists p 39
Allied Artists p 95
Chaplin/United Artists p 125
Cineguild/Rank p 37
Columbia pp 57, 69, 107, 107, 111, 123, 137, 169
Ealing pp 103, 109
Embassy Pictures pp 81, 139
Enigma Goldcrest p 113
EON/United Artists p 75
Goldwyn/RKO p 27
Hawk Films Prod/Columbia p 51
Ladd Company/Warner Bros p 31
London Films p 173
Lucas Film/20th Century Fox p 161
Lucas Film/Coppola Co/Universal p 15
MGM pp 25, 49, 127, 129, 131, 155, 175, 185
Miramax/Buena Vista p 143
Mirisch/United Artists p 91
Orion pp 47, 171
Paramount pp 35, 43, 53, 55, 73, 133, 141, 147, 167, 179
RKO pp 45, 99, 105
Sam Goldwyn/Channel Four/Close Call p 115
Selznick/MGM p 77
Stan Laurel Prods/Hal Roach-MGM p 181
Stanley Kramer/United Artists p 89
20th Century Fox pp 11, 67, 83, 119
Two Cities p 87
United Artist pp 9, 17, 19, 145, 157, 159
United Artists/Fantasy Films p 135
Universal pp 13, 59, 65, 97, 101, 151, 165
Wark Producing Company p 93
Warner 7 Arts p 183
Warner Bros pp 7, 23, 29, 41, 62, 79, 153
Warner Bros/First National p 117
Zoetrope/UA p 21